DRUMBEAT
Business Productivity Playbook

HOW TO *BEAT* GOALS
AND DISORGANIZATION

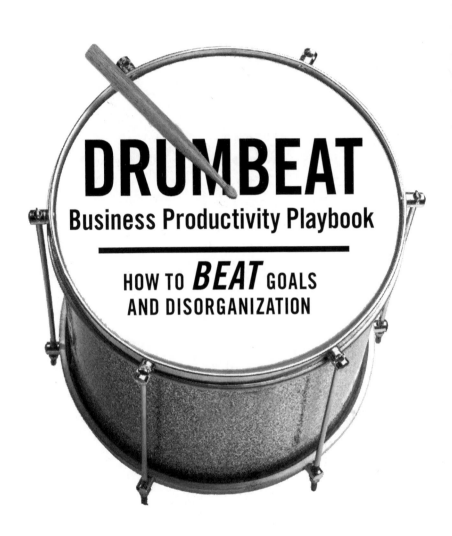

DRUMBEAT
Business Productivity Playbook

HOW TO *BEAT* GOALS
AND DISORGANIZATION

JONATHAN DENN

Drumbeat Business Productivity Playbook:
How To Beat Goals and Disorganization

Copyright © 2018 by Jonathan Denn. All Rights Reserved.

For information about this title or to order other books and/or electronic media, contact the publisher:

Success Full Press
PO Box 2078, Dennis, MA 02638
webite: DRUMBEATproductivity.com
email: successfull@drumbeatproductivity.com

Library of Congress Control Number: 2018901636

ISBNs: 978-0-9998918-0-3 (Hardcover) | 978-0-9998918-1-0 (pbk.) |978-0-9998918-2-7 (eBook) | 978-0-9998918-3-4 (audio)

Printed in the United States of America

Publisher's Cataloging-in-Publication data

Names: Denn, Jonathan, author.
Title: The Drumbeat business productivity playbook : how to beat goals and disorganization / by Jonathan Denn.
Description: Includes bibliographical references | Dennis, MA: Success Full Press, 2018.
Identifiers: ISBN 978-0-9998918-0-3 (Hardcover) | 978-0-9998918-1-0 (pbk.) |978-0-9998918-2-7 (eBook) | 978-0-9998918-3-4 (audio)
Subjects: LCSH Organizational effectiveness. | Business enterprises--Productivity. | Work environment. | Industrial management. | Success in business. | Management. | Business planning. | Strategic planning. | Time management. | BISAC BUSINESS & ECONOMICS / Management | BUSINESS & ECONOMICS / Decision-Making & Problem Solving | BUSINESS & ECONOMICS / Organizational Behavior
Classification: LCC HD56.25 .D46 2018 | DDC 658.5/15--dc23

TABLE OF CONTENTS

APPENDIX

PREFACE

*Are You Trying to Dance
Without a BEAT?*

I'VE ALWAYS LOVED ORGANIZATIONAL DEVELOPMENT. Don't know why. I majored in it in B school. Neuroscientists are rock stars. Master coaches are my heros. Can't explain it. I mean I love it like rock 'n roll or classic jazz or symphonies. I can't wait to take the stage and run a process. Better yet, design a process beforehand. It is what it is. I love this stuff. So . . .

Imagine this: You arrive home after work, smiling and feeling great. You're in control of your life, your job, and your business. You maintain your balance even in uncertain times.

You enjoy every work day. Planning is fun, and it's so easy it feels like second nature to you. You have a system and a mission. Your plans are flexible, not paralyzingly strict.

You don't react; you create. You don't obsess about the past; you learn from it. You complete tasks well and meet goals on schedule—*and* you feel deeply satisfied.

Sounds fantastic, doesn't it?

SO WHY DOES MANAGING YOUR DAY OFTEN FEEL LIKE DANCING WITHOUT A BEAT?

Why isn't your team more productive? Why are you spending most of your day reacting to problems instead of effortlessly creating results?

WHY CAN'T YOUR COMPANY ACHIEVE THE PRODUCTIVITY AND JOB SATISFACTION LEVELS YOU WANT?

Consider this: If everyone at your company was tapped into a relatable system that . . .

- maximizes thinking time
- minimizes information transfer time
- optimizes innovation processes

. . . wouldn't work feel more like play? With everyone on board and marching to the Beat of the same system, wouldn't time spent with your team and your customers be a *pleasure* instead of an annoyance or an interruption?

This book touts that kind of a system, and it comes with an irresistible backbeat.

THE DRUMBEAT productivity playbook is built for people who don't study productivity but can benefit from its innovative ideas. And that's probably everyone in your company.

Think about it. As crucial as productivity is, few companies communicate their proprietary systems in new employee orientation. The result? The group operates like orchestra musicians chaotically warming up before the conductor appears.

If you don't clearly set your own DRUMBEAT, your customers and your team will set it for themselves.

The DRUMBEAT in a symphony—and in the workplace—is the organizing principle that keeps the orchestra in time and laser-focused on its goal of making music. For your company, at its core . . .

- The DRUMBEAT presents a new way of thinking that leverages multiple tools for increasing your productivity and that of every member of your team.
- The DRUMBEAT's musical metaphors are simple enough for anyone to understand and execute. It keeps corporate jargon to a minimum. Would you rather have "jam sessions" with your team or unproductive meetings that drag on for hours? Would regular 90-minute "solo sessions" help you get your real work done for a change?
- The DRUMBEAT's framework brings rhythm to chaotic minds and company culture. It quiets the cacophony of everyday distractions.

When you, as the conductor, raise your arms to set the DRUMBEAT and cue that orchestral rhythm, the result is, well, beautiful music for everyone.

You don't have to know anything about music to use the DRUMBEAT System, it's just a metaphor to help everyone understand how all the parts fit together.

I've been fascinated with business productivity for most of my life. As I worked my way up the ladder to become CEO of a U.S. hotel chain, I observed everyone from the managers and team members to the purveyors and guests to see what was working—and what wasn't. I then co-directed an adaptive leadership program for 12 years and formally studied organizational behavior in business school.

Today, I'm the CEO of Drumbeat Productivity which provides team building, facilitation, organizational design, strategic planning, productivity coaching and workshops. I chair several monthly all-day board meetings for CEOs, business owners, and executives. I publish a weekly DRUMBEAT Blog, and do pro-bono mentoring with **SCORE**. But even with all this activity, I never feel rushed or harried. I spend most of my days in a state of flow: focused engagement. It's my DRUMBEAT.

Why the construct of a DRUMBEAT? When working with clients or presenting a workshop, I found the DRUMBEAT metaphor incredibly effective for any regularly practiced activity: newsletters, meetings, innovation time, you name it, and you will, too!

What does YOUR DRUMBEAT sound like? Let's find out.

INTRODUCTION
What's In Your Drum Kit?

To be supremely productive, you need to know where you're heading. It all begins with finding your personal focus—your driving Beat—that keeps you grounded, focused, and fully engaged. It also ensures you enjoy the journey.

But first: Why all the music references? Because music provides easily accessible metaphors that animate productivity strategies. No matter who's on your team, people from all backgrounds and education levels can take musical concepts and put them into action. **However, you do not need any musical knowledge or aptitude to use the DRUMBEAT Productivity Playbook, it's just a model in which to keep all this best practice.** Practice makes productive. I think the musical theme is cooler than corporate speak.

Tip: If you can't wait to up your productive game, go ahead and start playing with the DRUMBEAT Quick Start Guide in the Appendix.

Humans are hardwired for music. Studies show (and I've observed countless times) that people learn better, feel happier, and focus more when the right music is playing. It only makes sense: *Your brain has more receptors for music than it has for words.* This explains why the right Beat drives focus.

You ARE your music, but you need a DRUMBEAT. I'll even stretch and say that your team CRAVES a DRUMBEAT. With that in mind, let's start with an overview of what you're about to learn.

YOUR DRUM KIT

Your drum kit is based on hundreds of studies, proven neuroscience, countless books, thousands of one-to-one sessions with highly productive people, and decades of productivity experience (far beyond the 10,000-hour threshold). To these add attendance at marvelous workshops every month from those I've come to call "Doctorates in the Business School of Hard Knocks," a.k.a. Vistage Speakers.

Your drum kit (this book) includes all the tools you need to make big, positive, lasting transformations in your career and your organization. The steps include:

Setting the stage (Your Rallying Cry)
Defining what the customer hires the company to do (What's the Gig?)
Developing your goals (Big Bass Drums)
Setting 90-day professional goals (Rocks)
Setting 90-day personal goals (Roles)
Finding time to get it done (Rock & Roll)
Exceeding expectations (BEAT, the Goal)

Keeping an external record (Notes)
Deciding what to do and what not to do (Kettle Drum of
   Questions)

THE DRUMBEAT DAY

The DRUMBEAT Day centers around two 3-hour Sets comprised of 90-minute, 60-minute, and 30-minute Sessions each. The remaining time is for improvising. Here's just a glimpse into Sets and Sessions . . .

The two different kinds of efforts (Do-ing and Be-ing)
Practicing (Sets)
The four lengths (Sessions)
90-minute uninterrupted thinking Sessions (Solos)
60-minute communication Sessions (Jams)
30-minute maximum for rapid task completions (Finales!)
4-minute short tests/tasks (Warm-ups)

You'll also be part of:

Your own rhythm (Style)
The seven skills (Drums)
The next step (Beat)
When skills meet projects (DRUMBEATS)
Your main focus projects (STEEL DRUM)
Planning the next critical steps (Cymbal Crash-Throughs)
Your mental models and habits (Drumsticks)
How to plan your week (BEAT Sheet)
Measuring weekly progress (Counting Beats)
A no-lose situation (Win Storm)

Measures of nightly success (Scales)
Etiquette (Extensions)
Peer-to-peer coaching (Trios)
Places to be most productive (Venues)
Productivity tips (Drumroll of Riffs)

APPLYING YOUR DRUMBEAT

Every chapter in *THE DRUMBEAT* concludes with a review of that chapter's major Beats. Then there are three suggested formative tasks for you and/or your team to practice. There are also journal pages at the end of each chapter so you can take notes. Notes in music and journals are necessary and fantastically helpful.

The goal is to take away at least three major insights from each chapter that will change your life and the lives of those around you for the better.

WHAT TO EXPECT

The DRUMBEAT framework consists of habits and mental models based in neuroscience and packaged in a fun, easy-to-remember metaphor. It's a productivity system for those who aren't always linear thinkers and can get a bit "off-beat" from time to time. Which pretty much is everyone. Being off-beat is usually just a sign of someone being creative. Yet few companies leverage this powerful asset for business productivity. In fact, many unknowingly suppress their team members' creativity.

You'll discover at least 30 major elements, each with three main points and three Beats. These elements create a new neural network of 270 nodes with possible interactions, in mathematical terms of 270 factorial (270 x 269 x 268 x . . .

x 3 x 2 x 1 =). It's an unimaginably large number. (Just press 270 and then the drumbeat exclamation mark "!" key on your extended calculator to see this 270 factorial number.) If your neural network is larger then you'll achieve your goals faster by working smarter instead of just harder. Now, that's a beat worth dancing to, right?

When you put the DRUMBEAT into action, most team members individually become more productive. They become even happier as they produce better results with little or no aggravation or wasted time. Ideas and action plans will start sounding better because they will be better. And there WILL be more smiling because there will be more job satisfaction.

With the DRUMBEAT system in place, everyone in your organization gets a major neural pathway upgrade. As a result, your team and you will become (drumroll please) supremely productive!

PART ONE \\
SETTING YOUR STAGE

CHAPTER I

// Your Rallying Cry

WHEN YOU'RE AT YOUR VERY BEST, what's driving you?

When you find yourself "out of sync" and want to get back into your groove, what do you do to get there?

Think about these two questions for a several minutes. Take your time because this is important. Stop reading, go take a walk or look out the window . . . and think. The book will be here when you get back.

Got it? Now your task is to find a way to explain your answers so that no one will ever forget them, including yourself. This is your Rallying Cry—your driving motto—and it sets the stage for everything and everyone who is playing in your band.

Think about it. The first thing any band needs to know when they arrive for a gig is where the stage is—and how big it is. In the DRUMBEAT framework, your Rallying

1

Cry must be BIG—but it'll need to fit onto a small stage that you and others can remember and access anytime, anywhere.

YOUR THREE-WORD RALLYING CRY

You get three words to Set your Stage. If you're like most people, you're going to want a bigger stage and more words. But what's the point of a motto if no one can remember it?

Most people can remember three words. If you really need a fourth or fifth word, go ahead. But remember that your Rallying Cry must be short and succinct in order to be effective. It's got to capture the essence of what drives you and be as memorable as your ABCs.

You can change your Rallying Cry anytime you want. You may even need three Rallying Cries: one that's personal and only shared with loved ones, one that's professional to share with only your team, and another you reveal to clients and customers. The point is to build your DRUMBEAT Framework on your personal focus and drive.

HOW TO FORMULATE YOUR RALLYING CRY

Your Rallying Cry is your context. It should capture a feeling, an essence . . . something so important that no one will forget it. It must be applicable to everyone in your band—your team.

Consider these questions to arrive at your motto:

- What do you do well?
- What's truly unique about you?
- What's your single best character trait?

As an example, while writing this book my rallying cry words were: Create, Integrate, Tenacity. Here are those traits in motto form: "Create and Integrate with Tenacity." A few years ago my motto was, "Use Talents Enthusiastically to Host Growth." Lately, I've been using "Drum out Mediocrity."

Maybe your Rallying Cry is captured in a song. Maybe not. There are as many rallying cries and mottos and theme songs as there are people on earth.

Think of your Rallying Cry as your superpower autograph: the three words above your signature. One concept to consider might be that successful people don't quit as soon as unsuccessful people do. A good Rallying Cry motto for this superhero might be, "I'm not quitting!"

"Stay in Flow" was another Rallying Cry I used to produce this book. Psychologist Mihaly Csikszentmihalyi describes flow as what it's like to be fully engrossed, so that time flies; possibly as close as you can get to Be-ing the fullest expression of yourself. When I "Stay in Flow" I'm happy, less anxious, and living in the now instead of the past or the future. Flow has been associated with the feel good "alpha brainwaves."

Here are a few examples to help get you started on yours:

"THINK DIFFERENT."

—*Steve Jobs*

"LIFE IS GOOD."

—*Bert & John Jacobs*

"FAIL FAST AND OFTEN. FAIL CHEAP."

—*Seth Godin*

"THE ULTIMATE DRIVING MACHINE"
—*BMW*

"WE ARE GREAT!"
—*Tribal Leadership*

When you put the words down in writing, they become real—and powerful. They exist to consistently reaffirm your current opinion and goals, or they may raise doubts about your motivations. If that's the case, dig in again and find a new Rallying Cry that moves you.

Either way, having a well-honed Rallying Cry is always a win-win, and you cannot move to the next steps without it.

DEFINITIONS

So far we've been Setting your Stage. Now let's talk a little bit about setting the stage with some definitions of terms. In the DRUMBEAT Framework there are no employees or staff; those are work words. Once you find your DRUMBEAT, work becomes play. So, the two people you interact with the most, plus you, are probably your Trio. The rest of the people in your immediate area are your Band of Characters; if you are in a larger department or a smaller company, then your Team. The small "c" company is the business entity, the capital "C" Company are all the people; a Company of players.

\

CHAPTER REVIEW

To develop a strong DRUMBEAT to drive your career and business forward, you need to get in touch with what makes you an upbeat and productive person. If you can put that motivation succinctly into words, you'll have a Rallying Cry that picks you up when life tries to get you down. It will also set your own unique productivity stage to keep you focused and fully engaged. A strong Beat makes time fly. A Rallying Cry is your first stomp on the DRUMBEAT Stage, and it all starts with what makes you tick.

\|

THREE BEATS TO REMEMBER

\ You need a Rallying Cry.

| Your Rallying Cry is what makes you tick; it's what makes you YOU.

/ Your Rallying Cry will help you stay upbeat.

\|/

PRACTICE

Individuals

Come up with three Rallying Cries:

- One private for yourself or to share with your family.
- One professional to share with your team.
- One professional to share with your clients or customers.

This is an ongoing process. Stick with it. Once you have it, everything will seem clearer.

TEAMS/BAND OF CHARACTERS

Group discussion: Test out your Rallying Cry with your team or Band of Characters. Then co-create a Rallying Cry for your group as a whole. Let everyone chime in. Sleep on it.

Large companies

Group process: Repeat the two steps above, and bring the Team Leaders together to see how the Rallying Cries can be blended together for an over-arching Rallying Cry for the entire Company.

\ | //

RALLYING CRY NOTES

Use these pages to explore your personal, team, and public Rallying Cries.

TOP FOUR RALLYING CRIES

Ask your trusted advisors which they like best.
But you decide!!

1	2	3	4

CHAPTER 2

Dancing to the BEAT
of Your Inner Drummer

"IF A MAN DOES NOT KEEP PACE WITH HIS COMPANIONS,
PERHAPS IT IS BECAUSE HE HEARS A DIFFERENT DRUMMER.
LET HIM STEP TO THE MUSIC WHICH HE HEARS,
HOWEVER MEASURED OR FAR AWAY."

—*Henry David Thoreau*

THIS QUOTE GETS TO THE HEARTBEAT of your Inner Drummer. It's all about your personal drive and focus. You have to be able to identify and follow your passion. But you also have to stay focused on everything else that needs to happen, so as not to let your team down. The challenge lies in being able to accomplish both.

How do you keep your Beat while having to listen to everyone else's Beat? This is a question that's addressed throughout this book, starting with the next chapter on goal setting. But there's a step you must take after you determine your Rallying Cry—but before you start goal setting. That's the head game we call Your Inner Drummer.

Much has been written recently about the idea that people don't leave their jobs over money. Rather, they leave because they hate their boss, or because they don't feel empowered to make decisions. Your Inner Drummer needs to focus on behaviors that will keep you from being hated by your team or by your boss.

AGREEMENTS VS. EXPECTATIONS

"CREATING AGREEMENTS WORKS WONDERS. UP-VIBE YOUR PERSONAL AND PROFESSIONAL RELATIONSHIPS BY LEARNING TO CREATE AGREEMENTS INSTEAD OF EXPECTING OTHERS TO DO THINGS (AND THEN BEING DISAPPOINTED WHEN THEY DON'T)."

—*Steve Chandler*

As master coach Steve Chandler says: We need to create agreements instead of toxic expectations. Productivity is ultimately a two-way street.

If you're in a position of authority, you might simply tell a staffer to do something. Or you might explain the core values and then expect the team member to make the correct decisions. But when it really counts, it's best for both you and the team member to talk it through and agree on your respective obligations, with a date and time for completion.

Sounds easy enough, right? But how do you keep your Inner Drummer happily pounding away if you simply don't enjoy some of the tasks expected of you? One way is to squeeze the time out of the unpleasant stuff, and shift it to the fun stuff. Set a timer for the unpleasant tasks—and speed up that Beat. Really. Try it. It works!

The songwriting Sherman Brothers apparently have a deep understanding of the inner game of business. In this case "A Spoonful of Sugar" is your passion project—which, a little later on, you'll come to know as your "Steel Drum" project. Combined with many others, this technique will form a sustainable productivity system that will allow you to be confident in your efforts.

THE SOUND OF CONFIDENCE

Whether or not you're already confident and open minded enough to learn, a great way to help with the head game is to dive into the work of Alyssa Dver, President of the American Confidence Institute and author of *Kickass Confidence: Own Your Brain, Up Your Game.* I particularly like Alyssa's Key Confidence Indicators; transactional practices you can use to be more confident. Alyssa shows that confidence is a learned behavior—not something that's genetically handed out at birth.

Alyssa's work is based in the science of neuroplasticity. What this means is that the mind can grow and repair itself, a concept which disproves the long-held theory that the brain is somehow fixed and on a slow decline into oblivion. In fact, the brain can learn and grow at any age. What's wrong with being confident?

Absolutely nothing! In SWITCH: How to Change Things When Change is Hard, authors Chip Heath and Dan Heath use the Rider and Elephant metaphor coined by social psychologist and NYU Professor Jonathan Haidt.

In Haidt's illustration, the Rider has a destination, but struggles in trying to reach it. You're the Rider. Your company is the Elephant, pretty much going in whatever direction it wants. Obviously, trying to stop a moving elephant is difficult at best. But the Rider's goal is to get the Elephant to go down an acceptable path, hopefully with little or no destruction along the way.

In the DRUMBEAT Framework, your Inner Drummer is a lot like the Rider. The Elephant can refer to your company's culture. And as Peter Drucker, often called the founder of modern management, said: "Culture eats strategy for breakfast."

YOUR INNER DRUMMER'S THREE CHALLENGES

Challenge 1: Keep your BEAT no matter how slow it is at first.

The Inner Drummer's primary challenge is driving forward no matter how slow the Elephant.

Daniel Kahneman, Nobel Prize-winning economist, says most people make about the same number of good decisions. But really successful people usually have made one spectacularly good decision.

Keep an eye open for these opportunities. They're rare. But making great decisions is a fabulous way to get a stronger Beat going for your team. We'll discuss better decision models in Chapter 6.

Challenge 2: Be aware of what's holding you back.

Your Inner Drummer's second challenge is to manage default behaviors. Mel Robbins, author of *The 5 Second Rule: Transform your Life, Work, and Confidence with Everyday Courage,* calls default behaviors your Emergency Brake and Autopilot. The problem with these is that they hold you back from you being you! To crash through your emergency brake and autopilot's tendencies to keep you too safe to win more often, the DRUMBEAT Framework has Cymbals.

These Cymbals signify the moves you make in order to complete a successful strategy. In a band, cymbals demand attention with the sound of a crash. While our autopilot and emergency brakes want us to keep safely beating the drums, crashing through to the other side of an impediment is often necessary for a winning performance.

Challenge 3: Make sure your team can hear your BEAT.

The third challenge, using the Rider and Elephant metaphor, is to remember to pack the pachyderm chow to keep everything on track. The Elephant will always follow the food. In your DRUMBEAT Framework, you might think of this as, "you're drumming and you can't stop." We have to trick ourselves into using all the hot drums and cool crashes to get our points across to the team; we have to find a more danceable Beat.

YOUR INNER DRUMMERS' FOUR TOOLS

"...THE BRAIN IS LIKE VELCRO FOR NEGATIVE EXPERIENCES, BUT TEFLON FOR POSITIVE ONES."
— *Rick Hanson, Ph.D.*

Letting go of negative thinking and getting to the core of your own personal drivers is a crucial step in finding and maintaining your DRUMBEAT. I've found all of the following techniques very helpful, for myself and for many of my clients.

MEDITATION

Meditation can clear your mind in reasonably short periods of time. It's particularly useful when you're feeling overwhelmed or even confused. Meditation aids abound on the internet, so by all means, find what works for you. For many people, simply sitting quietly and focusing on breathing or listening to trance music are the easiest ways to meditate.

(Later in the book we'll go into great depth on the concept of Sessions. A Set is usually made up of a 90-minute Solo Session for deep work, a 60-minute Jam Session for meetings and communications, and a 30-minute Finales! Session for quick task completions. A 20 minute meditation period can easily be worked into the first and last or in-between.)

MINDFULNESS

Mindfulness practices and meditation are frequently confused. Meditation is meant to help you step out of the noise in your head, the beta brainwaves, by focusing attention on something neutral like your breath, sounds, or a word. Mindfulness is to be fully present in the moment without regret about the past or anxiety about the future.

We're hard-wired to avoid disasters, so we spend a lot of time worrying—instead of savoring the wonderfulness of each moment. While these feelings help us to survive, really high quality productivity comes from thriving in present activity. In DRUMBEAT Thinking, focusing on the present always results in a much stronger Beat than one masked by all the noise of the past and future.

SELF-HYPNOSIS

Another great way to control the head game is self-hypnosis. Hypnotists have long understood the effects of different brain waves. When your brain is in alpha waves, for example, you are bridging the gap to your subconscious, or what I call your CthinkO, or Chief Thinking Officer. Think of the C and O as ears, and "think" is what you do between them.

You are in alpha waves just before you fall asleep, and just when you naturally wake up. Meditation also has strong alpha wave activity. A good source for more information on self-hypnosis is *How Big is Your But?: Discover How to Finally Let Go of Blocks and Move Forward in Your Life* by hypnotherapist Renee Brent.

EMOTIONAL FREEDOM TECHNIQUE (EFT)

When feeling a bit off balance, EFT or Emotional Freedom Technique can be very useful. I've used this technique and have gotten great results on a number of occasions.

In a nutshell, you identify what's bothering you, acknowledge it, add an affirmation, and repeat both while tapping on meridian points. This can result in almost instantaneous calm. Could this calm be the result of the placebo effect? Well, if it works, does it matter? Declare victory, and move on to the next Beat. What do you have to lose? It's free, and it takes almost no time. You can also learn more from Nick Ortner's book *The Tapping Solution: A Revolutionary System for Stress Free Living.*

FIND YOUR POWER

You may be a career type person—you love what you do and can't wait to do it everyday. Or maybe you're a non-career type—you view your job as a means to get money that allows you to do what you really love.

Either way, in the DRUMBEAT Framework, your DRUMBEAT needs to be strong enough that people want to be around you.

In the next chapter, we'll discuss how your Inner Drummer overlaps with your Chief Thinking Officer (your subconscious). First you have to think. Then you have the power of your words and your actions—your Beat. Once you genuinely decide to get with the rhythm, it'll happen.

\

CHAPTER REVIEW

Your Inner Drummer needs a passion to drive you through all the boring tasks so that you can spend more time playing your fun drums. Your confidence plays a major role here, so don't take it for granted. Confidence is a learned behavior; it's not something you got (or didn't get) at birth.

There are three major opportunities to find your Beat. The Inner Drummer needs a general plan to help your Outer Drummer stop operating like one of those automated Beat machines. Your Inner Drummer also needs to stop stomping needlessly on the emergency brake anytime a change of tempo gets scary, and start stomping on the pedal of your big bass goal drums, which is up next.

\|

THREE BEATS TO REMEMBER

\ The Beat starts in your own head, nowhere else.

| Meditation and other techniques can help you tap your way to confidence.

\ Keep going, don't play it too safe, and amp your communication.

\|/

PRACTICE

Individuals

Inner Drummer Exercise: 15 Minutes

Of the three opportunities for helping your Inner Drummer—finding your passion, unearthing confidence in your abilities, and removing inner blocks—which is most challenging? What are you going to do about it?

Teams/Band of Characters

Share the essence and motivation of your Inner Drummer with two trusted people on your team. As mentioned in the introduction, Trio coaching is an effective way to turn boring work into fun, exciting play.

Large companies

Share the results of the Inner Drummer exercise with your boss, mentor, or HR director. Ask for their guidance, and ask them to share with you their own personal Inner Drummer challenge results.

INNER DRUMMER NOTES

What needs some practice?

INNER DRUMMER NOTES

What four notes would you like to play better?

1	2	3	4

PART TWO

YOUR BIG BASS DRUMS

CHAPTER 3

// Your Goal Drums

YOUR DEEP BASS DRUMS—and I mean really core-shaking—thunder "WHY?" and echo, "What's the gig?"

WHAT'S OUR GIG?

Why does your company exist? This is the core of your company culture. What's Our Gig? is based on the Jobs To Be Done theory of innovation, and the work of Clayton Christensen, Harvard Business School professor and Disruptive Innovation Expert. You can read more in his book *Competing Against Luck: The Story of Innovation and Customer Choice.*

In this construct, there are no products; there is only the product's value or service to the user. See if you can fill in these blanks:

"_____ hired us/me to _____ so s/he can _____.

It's not as easy as it looks. Forty different people may give you forty different answers.

Don't use the generic word "customers" in the first blank. Instead, be as specific as possible: parents, commuters, plumbers.

The second blank is the solution to the problem the hirer has: fix the broken pipes, end the boredom, save time. The third blank is how their problem is solved or the wonderfulness of the ending. Take some time to see if you can come up with three What's the gig? sentences.

Depending on the nature of your business, you might have to sort through dozens of these gig sentences. If so, group them into categories or personas to focus on your marketing messaging. For example, you can use this information to fine-tune your social media. (We'll talk some more on the topic of better-sounding marketing in Chapter 12.)

WHAT'S NOT OUR GIG?

Inverting this model is especially useful in the Innovation drum.

"_____ DOESN'T hire us/me to _____ so s/he can _____."

Ouch! What you learn here may lead you to change your behavior, or to go ahead and let the competition have those customers.

"STRATEGY IS KNOWING WHAT NOT TO DO."

—*Michael Porter, economist and business strategist*

YOUR COMPANY'S RALLYING CRY

In the previous chapter, you used the three to five-word game to define your own motto or Rallying Cry. Now let's try it for your company.

What does your company do best? What makes it unique? What emotion or verb speaks to the heart of what your company does? Tie those ideas together into a coherent statement. This may result in a motto you can use to inspire your Company, or as a slogan or tagline to enchant customers and attract future team members.

GOAL SETTING

Now that we've looked at the "Why?" of your company and its goals, let's move to the "When?"

Just like in David Bowie's song "Changes," reporters, like drummers, have to decide how and when to change their Beats. By the end of this chapter you'll be reporting some or all of your goals to yourself and perhaps others. It's crucial that you actually write them down on paper. Studies have proven that writing things out makes them real.

There is some controversy over the most effective lengths of time to use in goal setting. In Salim Ismail's *Exponential Organizations: New Organizations are Ten Times Better, Faster, and Cheaper Than Yours (And What to Do About It)*, one year is the maximum recommended time span. The rationale is that the world is moving so fast that by calendar's end you may have to change your goals entirely.

Ismail looks at several new successful platform companies in various industries. Some of these are now the largest in their sectors but they have very few hard assets. For example, AirBnB owns no hotel rooms and rideshare services own no limos . . . yet. How might your industry be affected if a new exponential organization entered the race? Could your company be that exponential organization?

Alternately, many other books on goal-setting recommend 1-year, 3-year, 5-year, 10-year, and even 25-year goals. There is good logic and reasoning behind each of these lengths as well. And as we'll explore in the Trios chapter, your company's goal lengths may be more a matter of your personal style than any science, art, spirit, or expert recommendation.

At the end of the day, it matters that your style aligns with your goals, or that your goals align with your style. My personal default is to look for times when the art, science, and spirit all align. It's a three-win Beat . . . a win-storm! When you can determine and fully understand your goals, lightening strikes!

The DRUMBEAT Framework goal defaults are a 3-year cheer and a 1-year track, with several 90-day Rock and Roles . . . Rocks being your business goals and Roles being your personal and non-business goals.

There are two kinds of goals: transactional and transformational. Transactional goals are managerial, measurable, monetary, and objective. Transformational goals are about leadership, inspiration, non-monetary, and subjective concerns.

To illustrate, let's look at one transformational goal and one transactional goal in each of these four bass drums:

3-year, 1-year, and 90-day, which includes both personal and company goals.

TRANSACTIONAL GOALS

- In 3 years: Be the industry-leading company based on growth rate.
- In 1 year: Beat industry average growth.
- In 90 days, company will: Increase revenue 10% year over year.
- In 90 days, I will: Be in a position to ask for a raise or increase owner's draw.

TRANSFORMATIONAL GOALS

- In 3 years: Be the thought leader in our industry.
- In 1 year: Define new core values for our company.
- In 90 days: Company will: Increase feelings of well-being and teamwork.
- In 90 days: I will: Become more upbeat through better diet, exercise, and sleep.

Once you set goals, you'll figure out the best, fastest, easiest ways to achieve them through the next set of drums.

(In Part Four, we'll discuss Converging on the Do-ing Snares and Diverging on the Be-ing Shells with a deep dive into management vs. leadership issues. You not only manage and lead your team but also yourself. This is a core value in the DRUMBEAT.)

WHEN A GOAL IS EXISTENTIAL

I talk with a lot of business owners. A common dilemma is whether they should grow by buying other businesses, hold on to the one they've got, or sell and cash out. If you are considering selling, keep in mind that doing it correctly and wisely is a process. Selling your business should be in your 3-year Bass Drum, not a shorter timeframe.

The most important question you can ask yourself in the buy/sell/hold conundrum is "Why?" If your answer boils down to not much more than escapism, it's probably not a great strategy. Use the Buy, Sell, or Hold (your business or career) exercise at the end of this chapter to gain clarity on your particular situation.

\

CHAPTER REVIEW

To really understand your goals, start by defining why you do what you do. The Jobs to Be Done theory is useful for understanding your company's gig and where it's taking you. Just as you have a Rallying Cry, your Company needs one to get beyond being just a place to work.

The goal is to be a place to share in success and have fun. Goal setting can be tricky, but it's a necessary step for fitting your Beat with everyone else's, as well as the company's. Once your goals are set, you can move on to the fun: Achieving them.

\|

THREE BEATS TO REMEMBER

\ Why do you do what you do?

| What is your understanding of what your company really does?

/ Listen for and list your measurable and transformational goals.

\|/

PRACTICE

Individuals

If you're like me, you probably have a bunch of different goals, so zeroing in on the important ones can be challenging. Try keeping a journal for a week and note any thoughts you have on this subject. At the end of the week, try the Gig exercises again and see if you can get some clarity.

Teams/Band of Characters

What's your department's gig? Run the Gig exercise for how you serve your larger team or the company itself.

Large companies

Determining the company's Gig can be a very challenging exercise. To break it down into simpler components, start by having everyone write up as many gig sentences as they can on sticky notes. Post them all on a wall. Now ask people to vote with a Beat mark "\" on the notes they feel are most representative of the company's purpose. Finally, tally the votes to choose the top four gig sentences. Your Company's idea of the company's gig might not be what you'd expect.

How does the Gig exercise inform the development of your company's internal Rallying Cry?

BUY SELL, OR HOLD? EXERCISE

If you are a fan of letters, literally and figuratively, you'll love this writer's exercise: Pretend it's twenty years in the future. Write two letters to someone you love: The first letter tells why you're happy that you sold your business or left that job long ago. The second letter explains your regrets for having sold your business or left your job.

Carry out both exercises, in an order that makes sense to you.

I've seen every possible outcome from these exercises. The point is to fill your Goal Drums correctly. The biggest mistakes happen when assumptions are taken as facts, so be sure to think through all possible assumptions clearly. Obviously there's no point in having a great strategy based on false assumptions. Just look at what that did for Kodak and Blockbuster.

\|//

YOUR BIG BASS GOAL NOTES

What's your Gig? What's your company's gig?

YOUR TOP 4 GIG POSSIBILITIES.

1   2   3   4

YOUR COMPANY'S TOP 4 GIG POSSIBILITIES.

1   2   3   4

TRANSACTIONAL GOALS

(You can measure it): List your top 3yr, 1yr, and 90 day rock and role notes in descending order, and at the bottom the first steps you need to take tomorrow to make them happen.

1	2	3	4

TRANSFORMATIONAL GOAL

(Best described in words and concepts): List your top 3yr, 1yr, and 90 day rock and role notes in descending order, and at the bottom the first steps you need to take tomorrow to make them happen.

1   2   3   4

CHAPTER 4
// The Kettle Drum of Questions

LIKE IN WHITNEY HOUSTON'S SONG "How will I know," how *will* you know what to work on next week?

Most productivity systems are basically glorified "to-do" lists. The problem with to-do lists is that they make all tasks appear equally important—which they never are. In fact, it's very similar to the way a computer would look at its day. What you get is a lot of white noise with no rhythm.

YOUR BEAT SHEET AND KETTLE DRUM OF QUESTIONS

For filling our Sessions, we pull items from the one-page BEAT Sheet menu which is fed from the Better Sounding Questions that bounce out of the Kettle Drum. This Kettle is your deepest-sounding drum, and the easiest way to set your DRUMBEAT because it's based on the most relevant notes and questions in your life and company.

Although artificial intelligence (AI) is becoming more prevalent in our lives and taking increasingly more jobs from us humans, we do have one major competitive advantage: the ability to ask great questions. Think about it. AI is really good at answering questions. But it's awful at asking questions. If you want to thrive in your job or see your business outpace the industry, you have to be fantastic at asking questions.

The Kettle's questioning heat raises up the best Notes above the white noise. Otherwise, how WILL you know what to do? Whoever asks the best questions wins.

THE THREE TYPES OF NOTES

With advances in neuroscience, we now know definitively that our conscious minds are terrible at remembering things. We only have limited recall capacity. While we can choose to use it for remembering to buy milk on the way home, it might be better to use this precious resource for deciding what, why, and when to do what's important. Put milk on the shopping list, get in the habit of checking the list when you know you'll be passing a store, and focus on the important stuff.

In the DRUMBEAT, we call these external memory items "Notes," as in musical notes. There are essentially three kinds of Notes.

1. Needs, or Need-Tos. What needs to get done soon. These can be personal or professional. Personally, I use my smart phone's shopping list for personal noise, and a couple of Kettle lists in its reminders. If I'm driving, I just give a voice command to add something to a particular list. If my phone's not around, I jot a note for distribution

later. I have a pen and paper everywhere I sit, and three journals in the car.

I put these need-to items in the 30-minute Finales! drum of my Daily BEAT Sheet. If I need someone else's input, I put it in the 60-minute Jam Drum. If it needs a concerted effort, I put it in a 90-minute Solo Drum (NO interruptions!). The drums look like circles on the Daily BEAT Sheet.

Here's an example of how to set up your BEAT Sheet Menu . . .

90-minute Solo Drum
Whitepaper concept and outline
Read research on assessment tools
Work on a new strategy for product X

60-minute Jam Drum
Discuss goals of a structured interviewing system with HR
Call 2 clients a week to find out why they went cold
Take one A player out to lunch each week

30-minute Finales! Drum
Get the forecast done by Wednesday
Quick call to a vendor about late deliveries
Decide between two new email services

Whether you prefer to do this analog in a journal and/or digital in the cloud is a matter of your personal style. The appendix has many different worksheets for you to try to find your favorite. You will pull from this menu to loosely plan your week, and specifically plan your day. So, tonight I might plan my morning Set to look like this . . .

Tuesday AM

90-minute Solo Drum session
Read research on assessment tools

60-minute Jam Drum session
Call 2 clients to find out why their volume decreased

30-minute Finales! Drum session
Quick call to a vendor about late deliveries
Decide between two new email services
If there is any time left check the BEAT Sheet menu for another quick task to knock off.

The point of the BEAT Sheet Menu is to separate out the important items from the rest, the Need-tos from the . . .

2. Wants. What you want to get done someday.

3. Mights. What interests and intrigues you.

For Wants and Mights, the same goes for capturing the external memory, but these are deposited into the bottom of the Kettle Drum of Questions for processing at the weekly BEAT Sheet review (or whenever I'm searching for a new project).

Whenever possible, write out your Notes as a sentence, not just as a single word or phrase. This way, you'll have a much better idea what you were talking about when transcribing them into the Kettle.

> "THE THING THAT JESUS REALLY WOULD'VE LIKED WOULD
> BE THE GUY THAT PLAYS THE KETTLE DRUM
> IN THE ORCHESTRA."
>
> — *J.D. Salinger, The Catcher in the Rye*

Good news, we all get to play our own Kettle drum. While you can use the one-page illustrated Drum Kit as a mind map and fill in many of the elements, the Kettle is for concept only. It's way too small. I use a text document as the master Kettle because it can grow quite large quite quickly.

I prefer to organize my Kettle Notes in folios. Anecdotally, prolific writers admit to using folio systems. The point being you may have a great idea for a future project, and this is where you capture it. Here's an example of what your Kettle Note section might look like . . .

E.g.

\\ FILTERING QUESTIONS //

\\ Notes //

MY BOOK
Chapter Outline
Possible Titles
Great Sentences
Etc.

IDEA FOR A NEW BUSINESS

What problem does it solve?

What are the personas?

What are the competitors missing?

Etc.

BUCKET LIST

See the Grand Canyon

Get a front row seat for the concert

What would be an epic trip for the family to remember?

Etc.

IDEAS FOR WORK

A new way to handle client files

Upgrade the CRM

New "touch" architecture

Etc.

BOOKS TO READ

Etc.

DIRECT REPORT: NAME

Etc.

Whenever a Note Folio becomes too wieldy I set up a separate Kettle just for that project. The point is to have one Kettle that helps you decide what to do and why, and others if needed for project work that requires you to do deeper thinking in the meantime.

Remember, you have limited conscious cognitive resources. Think of this process as mental hygiene. You take a daily bath or shower, or should, so try taking fifteen minutes a day to scan your notes to clean your mind of distracting clutter. If you are thinking about stuff at the bottom of the Kettle when you should be in a deep 90-minute Solo Session on another topic, scrub your mind of it. You'll get plenty of time to think about these other Notes later, maybe in the shower.

HOW TO CUT THROUGH THE CONFUSION

Now that you have all these Notes brewing in the bottom of your Kettle Drum, the next step is to determine whether these Notes can earn their way to the top of the Kettle for serious consideration.

Here's how to sort through them: If a Note is sufficiently interesting, move it to the top of the Notes section, just under the Filtering Questions section. Think of this Note as auditioning for the 7 Skill Drums, which is where you decide whether or not to work on something for next week. (You might want to bold or enlarge the fonts of Notes you don't want to forget. I find a whole page view to be quite helpful.)

FILTERING QUESTIONS

To promote a Note to the 7 Skill Drums (which we'll cover in detail in Part 4), you'll need to develop your own set of Filtering Questions. Here are a set of Filtering Questions for you to try. If they work for you, great. If not, create questions that do.

Is this worth my time?

Does this require that I have a Fixed Mindset (get it done!) or an Open Mindset (find an answer)?

Is it important, or merely urgent? Urgent tasks can be delegated, but only you can work on your important items.

Does it have to be done? Does it have to be done by me? Does it have to be done now?

I'm thinking of doing this for what preferred outcome? Is that outcome sufficient reward?

Why, why, why . . . Why? Ask yourself why you want to consider this. When you have answered that, ask "why?" of that answer. Keep asking yourself "why?" after each answer until you get to a natural conclusion. You will learn a lot about this Note by the time you're done, and it may easily be returned to the bottom of the Kettle. (Remember, you have more ideas than you can act upon. On another day, you might pitch the same Note to yourself and find it's the perfect time to promote it to the top of the Kettle.)

The Six Thinking Hats: First gather the data (White Thinking Hat), then acknowledge how you feel about the subject using three words (Red Thinking Hat), then identify the best case scenario (Yellow Thinking Hat) and the worst case scenario (Black Thinking Hat), then think outside the box for a creative solution (Green Thinking Hat), and finally define the next step (Blue Thinking Hat). This process is vastly superior to following only your gut (Red Thinking Hat) every time. You can read more about this process in *The Six Thinking Hats: An Essential Approach to Business Management* by Edward de Bono.

How does this Note fit into what's already in my 7 Skill Drums?

THE 7 SKILL DRUMS—A QUICK PREVIEW

Let's say you have heard a Note above all the white noise. Your Filtering Questions have found it worthy of promotion, and it has a perfect pitch. The next step is to phrase it as a question—a really good question.

Neuroscience studies show that the subconscious mind is exponentially more active than the conscious mind. Its currency is questions. In other words, you literally have an internal Chief Thinking Officer who requires no pay other than your conscious mind getting a good night's sleep, proper nourishment, staying hydrated, and sufficient exercise.

Your CthinkO loves a good puzzle. It takes a Note and transforms it into a quality question, like a caterpillar metamorphoses into a butterfly.

Sounds complicated? It's not. Here's an example. The note is "exercise more." You might ask the following Better Sounding Question on the top of your Kettle, "What exercise will I do?" Your CTO may have your answer for you in the morning. Try that.

In its new question form, your Note is ready to be placed in the top of the Kettle, and perhaps even in one of your 7 Skill Drums. The 7 Skill Drums are Learning, Innovation, Prediction, Strategy, Money, Enchantment, and Teamwork. It's almost impossible not to fit a really good question into one of these 7 Skill Drums, which we'll talk about more in Part 4.

For our "What exercise will I do?" the Money Drum is also known as the Execution Drum. If you aren't healthy, you can't make money. So you'd put it there until it becomes a habit and you can cross it off and make room for the next project.

Now write down any possible answers or interesting tangents to the question. When you're done, end with a question for your CthinkO. Then move on to something else; the brain likes to frequently change subjects.

Your Filtering Questions have done their job. Now it's your job to keep asking better questions. Warren Berger wrote a book on this subject, entitled *A More Beautiful Question: The Power of Inquiry to Spark Breakthrough Ideas*. The title comes from this quote . . .

> "ALWAYS THE MORE BEAUTIFUL ANSWER WHO ASKS THE MORE BEAUTIFUL QUESTION."
>
> —*e.e. cummings*

Perhaps the best question in Berger's book starts as "How might we . . . ?"

If this were phrased, "How should we . . . ?" it would imply that we need permission.

If it was "How could we . . . ?" it would imply that someone else was responsible for the decision, or that it might not be possible. If the phrase used "I" rather than "we," then it would infer the absence of a team.

For the DRUMBEAT, we rephrase it as, "You get stronger Beats from a Better Sounding Question." In this way, "sounding" means it is not only heard by the listener, but it also sounds solid to the listener. You know it when you hear it. Think of it this way: When you play the Kettle Drum well, you're *really* reaching everyone's eardrums!

EXAMPLES OF BETTER SOUNDING QUESTIONS (BSQS)

"How might I find more time to read so I can increase my effectiveness?"

"What kind of innovation processes exist to help us be more creative?"

"What's the economy looking like for our industry next year?"

"How can we start growing faster than our industry?"

"How might we improve our funnel and increase the percent of sales that we close?"

"What would make our customers fiercely loyal to us?"

"How might we become the employer of choice in our area?"

It's really difficult not to get into a really strong Beat with questions like these pouring out of everyone's booming Kettle Drums. The following is how you might set-up your digital Kettle Drum.

\\\ KETTLE DRUM OF QUESTIONS ///

\\ *Better Sounding Questions* //

E.g. How might we become employer of choice?
Ask the team over pizza
What do other industries do?

\\ *Filtering Questions* //

E.g. Is this important or merely urgent?
E.g. Should I do this or someone else?

\\ *NOTES* //

\ Sales Folio Notes /
E.g. Review step 2 in the funnel

\ Production Folio Notes /

Notes

Notes

Notes

Later, when we get to the weekly BEAT Sheet review, you'll be pitching these Better Sounding Questions to land in one of the 7 Skill Drums. Whether a question makes it or not depends on how worthy of your time it is. What's it not saying to you?

> "BUT IT'S HARD TO RESIST A GENEROUS QUESTION. WE ALL
> HAVE IT IN US TO FORMULATE QUESTIONS THAT INVITE
> HONESTY, DIGNITY, AND REVELATION. THERE
> IS SOMETHING REDEMPTIVE AND LIFE-GIVING
> ABOUT ASKING A BETTER QUESTION."
> — *Krista Tippett from* Becoming Wise:
> An Inquiry into the Art of Living

\

CHAPTER REVIEW

Most productivity systems center around the to-do list. The DRUMBEAT focuses instead on Notes in external memory, Filtering Questions, and Better Sounding Questions.

Our conscious minds are not good recording devices, so store Wants and Might Notes deep down in the Kettle where they can brew. Be wary that some Need Notes may merely be urgent, and not really worthy of your time; try delegating these.

If Notes at the bottom of the Kettle can pass through the Filtering Questions, then they are worthy to be interviewed for further promotion by a process of rephrasing the topic into Better Sounding Questions (BSQs).

You'll know when a BSQ is worthy of your time. Now that they're Beats, these former Notes are ready to bounce out of the Kettle to see the light of day on next week's BEAT Sheet! More on that in Part Four.

\\

THREE BEATS TO REMEMBER

\ Your chief thinking currency is Notes, which come in three flavors: Needs, Wants, and Mights.

\ The Needs have earned some of your thinking time. Save the others for later.

\ Notes get promoted through Filtering Questions for the opportunity to become Better Sounding Questions, which in turn might stall or get promoted to next week's BEAT Sheet.

\|/

PRACTICE

Individuals

Kettle Drum Exercise: 30 Minutes

Set up your Kettle text document with the three sections as shown in the template above. From bottom to top, these are: Notes, Filtering Questions, and Better Sounding Questions. Put 3–4 Notes in the bottom. Choose a handful of the provided Filtering Questions, or use all 7, or write up your own. Then see if any of the Notes make it to the top of the Kettle where they need to turn into Better Sounding Questions.

Teams/Band of Characters

Group Discussion: Errors & Omissions

Gather those banded together around your gig and decide which of the default Filtering questions don't work, and what new question should be added that are specific to your company and industry. Afterward, everyone will be on the same page with the same Filtering Questions to ramp up your team's productivity.

Large companies

The Wall

If you don't have a literal idea wall, set up a virtual one. Take a week to let everyone post Filtering Questions from scratch. The following week, edit the entries for clarity, and then have everyone rank their favorites. A discussion with "The Boss" is a cool way to see if you are in sync.

Why is asking Better Sounding Questions important? Think of it this way: What if Kodak or Blockbuster had promoted the "roll-out new technology" Note and had asked Better Sounding Questions? They would still be here, instead of getting the boot and becoming footnotes in business history.

KETTLE DRUM OF QUESTIONS NOTES

Experiment with setting up your Notes either free form, by Skill Drum, by Project, or by Direct Report.

KETTLE DRUM OF QUESTIONS NOTES

Start building your Filtering Questions. Check with your Team and compare filters.

PART THREE

YOUR BEATS & DRUMSTICKS

CHAPTER 5

// Drums + BEATS = DRUMBEATS

"IF YOU'VE GOT A PROBLEM, TAKE IT OUT ON A DRUM."

—*Neil Peart (Rush)*

AT THIS POINT, you have all these interesting Notes simmering in the bottom of your Kettle Drum. A few of these have made it through the Filtering Questions and have become Better Sounding Questions.

You probably can't wait to start playing with one of them. To do that, start thinking in Beats, Drums, DRUMBEATS, and Skill Drums.

YOUR DRUMBEAT

Think of your passion—or at least your craft—as the Beat. It's the future you want to create. When you play a Beat, you're completing a mini commitment. You're rewarded with a little shot of dopamine. Every journey of a thousand riffs starts with the first Beat.

Your Drums are skill sets; they're containers of intent. When you think about playing the Drums, you're dreaming—in a good way. You are rewarded with possibility. You're making sure that you are not neglecting a necessary skill that makes you well-rounded and more productive. Think about this for a moment, aren't the most successful people you know using all their skills? These are the A Players. Do you think they just use the ones that are fun or easy?

Now, when you add your Beats (your passion) to your Drums (your skill sets), you get DRUMBEATS: How you roll. In other words, when you anticipate your DRUMBEAT, you're setting a rhythm for yourself and those who can see, hear, and feel your focus and drive.

DRUMS

There are 7 Skill Drums. These are made up of three Do-Ing Drums plus four Be-ing Drums. Almost every Better Sounding Question that comes out of the Kettle will easily fall into one of these Drums.

In Chapter 15, we'll discuss The Steel Drum, your most important Beat for next week. But to be supremely productive, none of these 7 Skill Drums can be ignored for long. Each will have different priorities during any given Session, Set, day, week, month, or Rock and Roll quarter.

THE 3 DO-ING DRUMS

We'll go into greater detail in Part Four, but as an overview, the three Do-ing Drums are:

1. **The Money Drum** for taking care of business. Great business plans have failed because the founder ran out of cash. You can't forget to Beat the Money Drum.

2. **The Enchantment Drum** for inspiring your customers and clients. Terrific products never really got their market share because they didn't know how to inspire the buyer with the Enchantment Drum.

3. **The Teamwork Drum** for building a Company from your awesome bands of characters. A fantastic business will fail if the Band of Characters has a bad attitude and culture because you've ignored the Teamwork Drum.

THE 4 BE-ING DRUMS

1. **The Learning Drum** for being well informed. Not keeping up with industry advancements can make your products or services obsolete because you've ignored keeping time with the Learning Drum.

2. **The Innovation Drum** for creative solutions. If your competitor is more creative than you are, you may not have enough market share to remain viable. This can be avoided by banging on the Innovation Drum occasionally.

3. **The Prediction Drum** to map the near future. If you don't forecast properly, you may be drowning in inventory—or you may not have enough inventory to supply the annual rush. Skip all that by playing the Prediction Drum properly.

4. **The Strategy Drum** to decide what should be done. If you choose a faulty game plan, you may not get a second chance, so don't forget to hit the Strategy Drum.

So, let's say one of your Notes has made it past the Filtering Questions, and it's now a Better Sounding Question. You already know what drum needs to be played, and it's made your heart skip a figurative Beat. What happens next?

You now have a Beat in mind as a possible answer. You need to put it into your schedule for the coming week for its first Session. We'll take a much closer look at your weekly BEAT Sheet in Chapter 16, but here's the theory.

PLAN YOUR DRUMBEAT

One stroke on the drum does not a DRUMBEAT make, so you need to plan the next three or four steps. One Beat is a great idea . . . an inspiration . . . the thing to do. . . . But now you have to plan out the DRUMBEAT.

Three Beats is a steady waltz, four Beats is more pop rock. Either will work for planning your DRUMBEAT. It's the same for many different types of strategies. Master chess players see the board serially in about four move chunks. They are looking for a decisive advantage in one of the sequences. Professional billiard players consider which side of the fourth ball they want to be on in order to have the next four ball run.

DRUMBEAT PLANNING APPROACHES

To be a master productivity drummer, you too need to think in three- or four-Beat riffs. This is how a Beat turns into your DRUMBEAT. The DRUMBEAT executes the plan, sets a rhythm for your Band of Characters, and most important, sets a rhythm for yourself.

1. **Three Act Play.** One model you might find useful is the Three Act Play, a strategy-down approach that follows Aristotle's Form of Introduction, Complication, and Resolution. In this form, you state the premise, identify the challenge or opportunity, and set the objective.

2. **Bottom Up.** Another approach is to identify the resources that you need, assemble them, and then determine who in your Band of Characters can be relied upon to take the task to completion.

3. **Brainswarming.** A third approach is a combination of the previous two, in a process known as Brainswarming, developed by Dr. Tony McCaffrey. When a path forward is not readily apparent, gather your Band of Characters together to whiteboard strategies at the top and resources at the bottom. See if your team can reach a "eureka moment" that connects the two.

In one Brainswarming video illustrating the process, the problem is ice on power lines during an emergency. The goal is to remove the ice from the lines safely. The strategies are blowing, shaking, or melting the ice. The resources are fans, hammers, and heaters.

A team member in this case is able to connect the dots: She suggests flying a helicopter—essentially a portable fan—over the wires to remove the ice. Now there's a riff for you!

The next step in this process is the follow-up: Where can we find a helicopter? Who will fly it? How much will it cost? I'm a BIG fan of small tests, and you should be too. For example, before buying a helicopter, let's figure out how we can try a limited test to see if the helicopter solution will actually work.

Brainswarming is essentially a mental model, a tool used to solve problems. So while you're planning your three or four DRUMBEAT riffs using Better Sounding Questions, you can only make noise if you have Drumsticks. We'll take a close look at the two Drumsticks, Mental Models, and Habits in the next chapter.

> "IF DRUMSTICKS ARE FOR PLAYING DRUMS,
> YOU WOULD THINK THAT BREADSTICKS WOULD BE FOR
> PLAYING BREAD, WOULDN'T YOU? "WOULD YOU LIKE SOME
> BREADSTICKS?" "NO, THANK YOU, I DON'T PLAY BREAD.
> I PLAY DRUMS. PERHAPS I'LL HAVE A DRUM ROLL."
>
> — *George Carlin*

\

CHAPTER REVIEW

A Note is a wannabe Beat after making it past your personal Filtering Questions. A drummer bounces the note out of the Kettle with striking questions to catch a new Beat. But a single Beat has no rhythm; it's just a noise in your head. It becomes a DRUMBEAT when you string together the next steps. Once you have three or four steps planned out, you have a DRUMBEAT that will focus your drive and get your Band of Characters in sync.

\\

THREE BEATS TO REMEMBER

\ Once you've identified a Better Sounding Question, you have a Beat.

| Plan the Beat's next few steps, and your DRUMBEAT will have that irresistible rhythm.

/ Mental models are helpful for planning your next moves.

\|/

PRACTICE

Individuals

Identify one of the 7 Skill Drums that you think needs the most attention. Perhaps it's empty or almost empty. Now look through your Notes and see if there is a possible solution simmering in there. Can the Note make it past the bouncers and be something worth playing?

Teams/Band of Characters

Hold a monthly meeting to discuss the Better Sounding Questions that each of your Band of Characters is considering for their DRUMBEAT. How does it fit into your collective DRUMBEAT? How might they all fit together?

Large companies

Have each department head do the previous exercise with their teams, and bring the three most interesting ideas to a C-Suite meeting; perhaps the most interesting, the most creative, and the most do-able. Another good possible trio might be: the highest upside reward, lowest downside risk, and best reward/risk ratio.

\|//

NOTES FOR BETTER SOUNDING QUESTIONS

(What Notes are worthy of turning into a question to start filling up your Skill Drums)

CHAPTER 6

// Drumsticks to Get Unstuck

DRUMS ARE PRETTY. They're shiny. They're cool. But they're not all that useful without drumsticks. In fact, having a drum without drumsticks is kind of like having a book but not enough light to see the phrases.

In the DRUMBEAT, you have two drumsticks: mental models and habits. You might think of these as "what" and "how." Or you might come up with your own nicknames for these drumsticks.

Whatever you call them, knowing how to deploy your mental model drumstick and your habits drumstick is the only way you can actually play that shiny, pretty drum. Here's how, starting with mental models.

MENTAL MODELS

Mental models are little "rules" of life, truisms, good ideas to follow, when-in-doubt scripts, default thought patterns. . . . Essentially these are thinking patterns that help you maneuver successfully through life.

After hundreds of thousands of years of hunting, gathering, and doing our best not to be preyed upon, our species has become hard-wired to conserve energy. But conserving energy and being lazy are two very different things. With good mental models, many difficult tasks can become easy habits.

In his book THINKING, FAST AND SLOW, Daniel Kahneman calls this "Type 1" and "Type 2" thinking. Type 2 thinking requires extra effort and blood sugar; that's why we develop mental models to automate what we do repetitively. But here's the rub: We need to continually upgrade our mental models to keep up with our rapidly changing society.

One example of Type 1 thinking is the way our subconscious minds handle a good deal of our driving. The fact that you probably drive every day without bumping into anything or breaking any laws is because your subconscious actually does most of the driving. That's why you can do some pretty good Type 2 thinking in the car. You might even ask yourself a Better Sounding Question before shifting the car—and your brain—into drive.

Mental models have been discussed since the beginning of time. Ancient texts suggest ways of thinking at certain times. Philosophers write about better ways of thinking. In popular TV culture, Agent Gibbs on "NCIS" has dozens of rules to live by, and they're numbered. Even modern science has studied how we're hard-wired to act, and only our mental models and Type 2 thinking can break that programming if we want to change.

Some models conflict with or modify others, so context is important. But all of these are mental models. A great place to search for new mental models to explore is the *Farnam Street Blog* by Shane Parrish.

HABITS

The other drumstick is made up of your habits. Mental models can only do half the job; they help you know what to do, and when. In order to actually use these models, you have to change the ingrained behavior patterns that are keeping you busy doing something else.

You might even say that while the Mental Models drumstick is your be-ing, the Habits drumstick is your do-ing.

> "YOU'VE GOT TO BE BEFORE YOU CAN DO, AND DO BEFORE YOU CAN HAVE."
>
> — *Zig Ziglar*

The reason it sometimes feels hard to change old habits is simple: Your subconscious mind is trying to conserve your energy—a little too much. So remember, every campaign begins with the first Beat of the drum. The same applies to establishing new, better habits, but only if you can tap the first routine change, and then add more Beats.

Try a new way every once and awhile. For example, Productivity Tip #12 below is: Read with Your Ears! Start with Charles Duhigg's book, *The Power of Habit: Why We Do What We Do In Life And Business*. The basic process here is a habit loop of Cue, Routine, and Reward. To successfully change a habit, the cue and reward stay the same but the routine has to change.

THE DRUMROLL OF PRODUCTIVITY TIPS (RIFFS): MENTAL MODELS AND HABITS

Another important reason to use both our mental model drumstick and our habit drumstick is to overcome our hard-wired biases. It's unscrupulous, but sometimes people use our cognitive biases to get us to do things that are against our best interests. Robert Cialdini, author of *Influence: The Psychology of Persuasion*, has written extensively about this, and we'll give more attention to this concept momentarily.

In the meantime, what follows is a list of mental models and habits for you to test to see whether they fit into your drumming style.

Note: The mental models are the odd numbered items and are written in the form of a question. The habits are the even numbered items, written in the form of an exclamation.

#1 WHAT SHOULD I BE DOING RIGHT NOW?

If you could have only one mental model, this would be it. I first asked myself this question in my twenties, when I was an assistant hotel manager. I never stopped. If you always do the most important tasks first, you'll always get them done, and something good is bound to happen.

#2 IN THE TIME IT TOOK TO WORRY ABOUT IT, IT COULD'VE BEEN DONE!

Why worry about something for weeks when you could take care of it with a quick phone call? Just take the first tap of that drum. Get started. Don't over-think an under-task. In the hotel industry, we used to call this the "a la minute." It can and should be done in the minute it's needed—not before, and not after.

#3 WHEN IN DOUBT, WHAT'S THE QUESTION?

If you don't know the way forward, you probably haven't found or asked the Better Sounding Question. Keep asking. You'll know what to do when you've asked enough questions. If you need to, go back to Chapter Four: The Kettle Drum of Questions to review how to dig deeper to find those BSQs.

#4 BEFORE GOING TO BED, ASK YOURSELF A QUESTION!

Your subconscious mind—your Chief Thinking Officer—is waiting to be fed. It eats questions while you sleep. Asking yourself a question is THE habit to add to your good night routine.

I usually look at the top of my Kettle for a few minutes before brushing my teeth. By the time I turn down the bed, the CthinkO is already turning over the topic. Even if I don't formulate a question, just looking at the list of Better Sounding Questions usually gives me something to jump out of bed for in the morning.

#5 CAN YOU EXPLAIN IT IN A WAY THAT A CHILD COULD UNDERSTAND IT?

If you feel strongly about a position or fact, then you should be able to explain it simply or write about it succinctly. If you cannot, then you may be a victim of someone else's propaganda. In that case, you might want to think it through for yourself by asking yourself the great countering question: "Can you help me understand why...?" based on the Feynman Technique, which is easily found with an online search.

#6 DON'T LET ANY NOTES GET AWAY!

Carry paper and pen. Better yet, get journals. Learn how to use your voice recorder. Practice using your voice command pals. Set up a Kettle on your smart phone. Put paper and pen everywhere you sit, stand, or lie down. If you don't let any of your Notes get away, chances are better that one might turn into a Better Sounding Question.

#7 COULD THIS BE A SPECTACULARLY GOOD DECISION?

As stated in Chapter 2, Nobel prize winner Daniel Kahneman writes that most people—both successful and not-so successful—make about the same number of good decisions. But only successful people have usually made one spectacularly good decision.

See if you can find your spectacularly good decision whenever you're considering a challenge or an opportunity. Is it lurking in there somewhere? A Win Storm first step? There frequently is, but it takes effort to discover it. Do you and your team have a big enough time stage? Can you and your Band of Characters budget Sessions for it, over a set period of time?

#8 GET AT LEAST ONE 90-MINUTE SOLO SESSION IN EACH DAY!

To read up on all the science behind this, try DEEP WORK by Cal Newport. During a Solo Session, there are no emails, no phone calls, no interruptions, and no auto-notifications. Put a red or yellow circle (drum) on your door to let your Band of Characters know to come back later if they need something.

This means you must have agreements on the rules for interruption. If you are doing innovation or creative work and need to surf for inspiration or combinatory play, just be sure you don't fall down any rabbit holes. Stay generally on the same topic. You'll be amazed at how quickly your thinking and productivity will improve.

Solo Session Variation: There is a process and book called *The Pomodoro Technique* by Francesco Cirillo. Set a timer for 25 minutes, followed by a 5-minute break. Do 3 of these in a row. 3 Pomodoros = a 90-minute Solo Session. There is good science, as well as anecdotal evidence, that these frequent 5 minute breaks bring fresh insights and don't decrease productivity.

#9 HOW CAN WE UPGRADE OUR HIRING PROCESSES?

We humans are spectacularly bad hirers. Get a system, stick to it, and upgrade as needed. Read up on best practices for hiring. There are a lot of studies being done, and someone in your organization needs to have them in their Learning Drum. Hint: The scale is tipping toward science and away from gut instinct. Investigate assessments.

#10 GET GREAT SLEEP!

Your brain needs sleep to repair itself. If you aren't getting good quality sleep, put "How might I get 5 REM periods a night?" in your Learning Drum. Set up a DRUMBEAT for testing new sleeping strategies. Be methodical. There's a ton of advice out there. Some will work for you, some won't.

Personally, I had a major improvement by using a grounding half sheet. I know other folks who wear yellow glasses to filter out blue light in the evening. And still others had significant improvements when they stopped reading or watching TV in bed. Recently Debra Wein, CEO of WellnessWorkdays. com told me just five minutes of stretching and deep breathing before getting into bed works wonders.

Dr. Andrew Weil has a breathing technique called 4–7–8. Take a deep breath in for a count of 4. Hold for 7. Blow out gently for 8. Repeat until relaxed. I call this "Sleep Weil."

#11 HOW DO YOU LEARN THE OTHER SIDE'S ARGUMENT BETTER THAN THEY DO?

> "I NEVER ALLOW MYSELF TO HAVE AN OPINION ON
> ANYTHING THAT I DON'T KNOW THE OTHER SIDE'S
> ARGUMENT BETTER THAN THEY DO."
> — *Charlie Munger*

Probably by allotting some practice time in every week with your Learning Drum.

#12 READ WITH YOUR EARS!

When in doubt read, and when you can't use your eyes try listening to audio books while working out, driving, and doing chores. You might just get a really clean house, too, if you're listening to a really good book.

#13 HOW CAN I GET STUCK IN A WIN STORM?

Instead of spending an hour on social media, why not start a white paper on a topic on which you have expertise? It's a no-lose proposition. You win by simply thinking something through thoroughly. You win if the boss likes it. You win if it ends up in your company's digital marketing stream. You win if it gets you a bigger raise. And you really win when that leads to an even more interesting topic! What's your win/win/win/win storm?

#14 NEVER ASCRIBE TO MALICE WHAT CAN BE EXPLAINED BY INATTENTION!

To observe the true brilliance of the Hanlon's Razor mental model, listen to people's reactions about other people's reactions or inactions. Some people default to malice, while others to inattention. It's a barometer of emotional intelligence.

Make it an intention for a day to notice which defaults are generally more successful, productive, and have a stronger DRUMBEAT. If you go to malice, you're operating out of your reptilian brain—the amygdala—not your entrepreneurial frontal lobe.

#15 HOW DOES TALKING TRASH HELP YOUR PRODUCTIVITY?

Only you can answer this for yourself. But here's a clue: While you're trash talking—what's not getting done on your BEAT Sheet?

In *The Seven Habits of Highly Effective People: Powerful Lessons in Personal Change*, Stephen Covey talks about the differences between your Circle of Concern and your Circle of Influence. Trash talking or gossiping comes in three forms: Listening to others trash talk, trash thinking, and trash talking yourself. But if you can stay away from this Circle of Concern and focus instead on your Circle of Influence (what you actually have the power to affect), you'll have a really easy mental model to stop trashing your career.

#16 STOP MULTITASKING!

Multitasking doesn't work. I'm not talking about the staccato Finales! in a 30-minute Session that we'll discuss later. Now, if it takes just a few minutes to complete some rote tasks, and you're a really good task juggler, go for it. I'm also not talking about listening to an audiobook while working out or driving. That's actually maximizing Type One and Type Two thinking.

But what I am talking about is serially juggling your focus over long stretches of your day, or week, or life. Don't do that quick check of social media or email. Group your calls for 60-minute meeting Sessions, and subgroup calls on similar topics.

Studies have shown that it takes ten to twenty minutes to get fully back to speed on each interrupted task. It's damaging your brain and your career. You're killing your productivity.

Multitasking is for deadbeats. You're sabotaging your life. Stop multitasking!

#17 WHY NOT GET UP EARLY?

Let's look at this question in our Sets format: If you don't get up 4 minutes early and walk around your home in complete quiet, you might NOT have a thought that will totally keep you focused for the whole day.

If you don't wake up 30 minutes early and use that half-awake half-sleep state lying in bed and thinking about your day, you might miss out on a creative solution that will amaze your Band of Characters. Hint: Ask yourself A Better Sounding Question.

If you don't get up an hour early, you'll miss out on getting some quality exercise that will give you all those great hormones to make you more upbeat, literally and figuratively.

If you don't get up 90 minutes early, you won't get that Solo Session in on your long dreamed-of creative project. This is how the DRUMBEAT got written.

#18 BE A BIG FAN OF SMALL TESTS!

Chocolate is good. Cabbage is good too. But no one has ever ordered chocolate covered cabbage in a restaurant. This is known as false equivalence. If you substitute the cabbage with cherries or coconut, you're a genius. That's true equivalence.

Logic matters . . . but results matter more. Before committing to a business plan, run a ton of little tests to see what happens. If your dogs don't eat the pet food, it's not a viable product no matter how logical the recipe seems.

#19 DOES UPBEAT PLAY BETTER FOR YOU THAN DOWNBEAT?

Before talking, think about what needs to be said and how you can say it with a positive upbeat mental attitude. People will enjoy being around you. Happy people are more productive in the long run.

#20 MIND MAP!

Simply thinking things through is often not enough. We'll dive deeper into this in Chapter 7: The Learning Drum, where we'll talk about three different learning styles: audio, visual, and kinetic. Depending on the kind of learner you are, you might listen to words in your head, but sometimes you might need to see them in abstract representation in order to reach a breakthrough. Draw it. This is why using mind maps regularly is a great habit to start.

Stay tuned, we'll be adding more to the Drumroll of Productivity Tips and Riffs soon. Here's one right now.

\

Bonus Productivity Tip: Instead of reading an email and responding with what interests *you*, try a greeting at the top followed by "Convo Below" then respond to their questions in order by breaking into their text with your answer. It will eliminate any confusion, make it seem like you are actually having a conversation, and make them feel as if you are really listening to them—because you are.

\

CHAPTER REVIEW

Without the two Drumsticks of Mental Models and Habits to whale on the Skill Drums, all we can do is stomp on the pedals of a few Big Bass Drums and brag. Goals without an action plan are useless. Neither will give you a supremely productive Beat. Like the Filtering Questions in your Kettle, find the Mental Models and Habits that will make achieving your goals easier and more enjoyable. As you upgrade your Mental Models and Habits, you'll begin to make much better decisions and be rewarded with fantastic results.

THREE BEATS TO REMEMBER

\ Developing your own Mental Models will make decision-making easier.

| Starting a new, good Habit is the easiest path to success.

/ Your DRUMBEAT'S strength depends on your Mental Models and Habits.

\|/

PRACTICE

Individuals

Start by identifying one new Mental Model to try this week. Then identify one new Habit riff for a routine this week. Keep Notes of other Mental Models and Habits you might experiment with in future weeks.

Teams/Band of Characters

Group Discussion: After the first week of individually trying the Habit and Mental Model of the Week, have a group discussion about what worked and what didn't. This is a Mental Model called a Plus//Delta.

Large companies

Gather the department heads to report on the small wins from the weekly Mental Models and Habit discussions. Are themes developing? Any new core values, roles, and activities worth testing?

\|//

Mental Model Notes

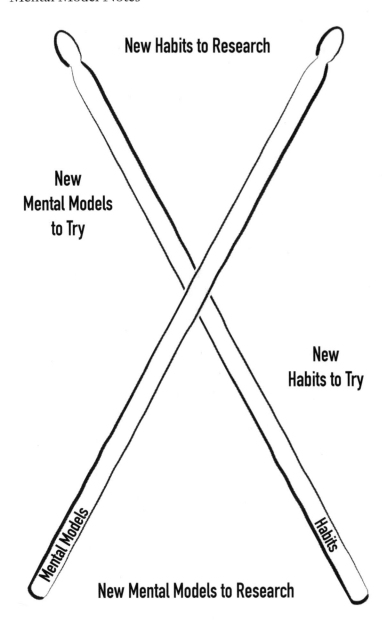

New Habits to Research

New
Mental Models
to Try

New
Habits to Try

Mental Models

Habits

New Mental Models to Research

PART FOUR

YOUR SKILL DRUMS

Generally speaking, everything that comes your way will require seven basic skill sets. This is loosely based on the work in Foresight University's *Foresight Guide*.

LIPS MET: THE 7 SKILL DRUMS

Late in the writing of this book, it occurred to me that it would be beneficial to provide you, kind drummer, with an acronym to remember the names of the seven Skill Drums. I looked at the names of each of the 7 Skill Drums, and behold: LIPS MET! (If you are the kind of person who prefers action over words, then reverse it into MET LIPS.)

MET LIPS? How poetic! How serendipitous! About 9 out of every 10 songs are about love. Many movies end when two people seal their love with a kiss. And they all have a strong Beat. In the DRUMBEAT'S 7 Skill Drums we refer to this as "When Do-ing met Be-ing."

Another good use for the LIPS MET acronym is as a reminder that you can't truly hear until your lips are closed. In other words, talk less—and listen more.

Note: Shells and Snares are types of drums.

LIPS: The Be-ing Shell Drums

The Be-ing shell drums are the LIPS:
Learning Drum,
Innovation Drum,
Prediction Drum, and
Strategy Drum.

Being shells, these also serve as protection. By helping you fully prepare before taking action, these Be-ing Skills have the Do-ing Skills' backs covered. They require significant thought, reflection, and practice—and they require you to answer four key questions:

What are you reading?
What could we do?
What might happen?
What should we do?

In other words, when you do your homework, you are far less likely to end up with disastrous results.

MET: THE DO-ING SNARE DRUMS

Moving on to the next part of the acronym, we find the Do-ing snare drums:

Money Drum,
Enchantment Drum, and
Teamwork Drum.

This is MET . . . and I'm so glad we have! Snare drums can also be referred to as trap drums or traps. Think about it: Your Teamwork must trap Money and customer demand (through Enchantment).

These three snare drums require pragmatism, efficiency, and excellence. Their three questions are:

How do we make money?
Who do we inspire?
How do we win together?

The Be-ing shell drums are for diverging on different facts, viewpoints, and variables. The Do-ing snare drums are for converging on the actions that need to be taken to get the desired outcome.

Together they constitute a fully functioning company.

WARNING

If you are always busy Do-ing, that's nothing to brag about. In fact, it's a sign that you don't know how to manage your commitments or productivity.

Clocks have a terrific Beat; the seconds tick away in perfect rhythm. But while clocks manage time, we humans can only manage our thinking, words, and actions—our DRUMBEAT.

The Chicago Transit Authority's song "Does Anybody Really Know What Time It Is" could've been the theme song for the disastrous downfalls of Blockbuster and Kodak. Both companies could have greatly benefited (and would probably have survived) with a lot more Be-ing.

On the other hand, if you are too busy Be-ing, nothing will get done. This is also known as "paralysis by analysis." In fact, many small decisions are so similar that it makes no real difference which one you choose. Just get on with it!

DIVERGING WITH THE BE-ING SHELLS

The world is changing at breakneck speed. That's why we need to keep learning. Every day, new Innovations are creating (and destroying) processes and businesses. Therefore, we need to be aware enough to respond proactively. The ability to see into the future with Prediction models gets easier with practice. And when enough attention is paid to these three shells, we can fill them with a winning Strategy.

Let's take a closer look at each of these Be-ing shell drums.

CHAPTER 7

// Learning Drum
Moving from Student to Virtuoso

WIKIPEDIA ATTRIBUTES THE FOUR STAGES OF COMPETENCE to Noel Burke of Gordon Training International. The learning journey begins with being Unconsciously Incompetent; we'll call this level of learning the Student. The next step is Consciously Incompetent, and we'll call these folks Amateurs. Once someone moves to Consciously Competent, we have ourselves a Maestro. And when that person achieves Unconscious Competence, we have a Virtuoso in our band.

Personally, I'm spectacularly stupid right up until the moment the Beat is truly heard. This is the moment that occurs between Student and Amateur. That's because learning is actually a process of setting up new neural pathways in your brain. It makes sense; you simply can't cross or sing a bridge until it's been built.

HOW YOUR LEARNING DRUM WORKS

Once you get used to the discomfort of not knowing the answer to a question, the payoff is an exquisite moment when the pathways connect. This is when you begin to hear your inner voice whispering—or rockin' out the possibilities.

Neuroscientific studies show that discomfort signifies the chaos of our brain's frontal lobe when we're trying to make sense of new information. Once the brain makes that connection, it chunks the new information together and sends it off to the diffuse parts of our brains (the subconscious, our CthinkO) to integrate. This is the Learning Drum.

READ!

When you're in doubt or feeling "stuck," go read something so that your frontal lobe can work out the problem. (At the time of this writing, I had six books started on my e-reader, over ten on the bookshelf by my chair, eight on my smartphone, and over a dozen audio books in progress.)

I read to be inspired. I read to get unstuck. Reading leads to an inspirational life. And it's almost impossible not to be supremely productive when you're deeply engaged with your life.

In Chapter 6, Drumsticks to Get Unstuck, we discussed replacing some social media habits with reading or writing habits. Obviously you know reading is important, or you wouldn't be reading this book.

When you read, you are accessing a virtuoso's deep work to upgrade your own neural pathways. It's a lot quicker and easier to learn many concepts, skills, and ideas from a book. Others are best learned through experience, as in case studies from those I call the Doctorates in the B School of Hard Knocks: the Vistage speaker bureau.

AUDIO, VISUAL, AND KINETIC LEARNERS

This leads us to another trio of characters: Audio learners, Visual learners, and Kinetic learners, a.k.a. "AVK." I haven't found a better book on the subject than *Collaborative Intelligence: Thinking with People Who Think Differently* by Dawna Markova and Angie McArthur. There are an amazing number of tools in this tome. Go bang on THAT learning drum for a while.

Here's one practical way to utilize AVK in your Teamwork Drum. If your Band of Characters are visual learners (V), meaning they learn best by reading, seeing a demonstration, or watching a video, then barking orders at them may not get the job done. Any misunderstandings are on you, not them. If you hired or inherited visual learners, you have to manage them visually.

Likewise, if your team are kinetic learners (K), they need to test and tinker in order to literally and figuratively get a feel for something. If you hand them an unreadable instruction manual, walk away, and find that things don't go well, then again, that's on you.

What if your team are primarily audio learners (A)? They might really benefit from the sound-based nature and analogies of this book. So if you send them a cryptic email and the job doesn't go well, then yes, once again, that's on you. You have to take the time to talk it through with audio learners.

It's not going to go well if you don't pay attention to how your team learns. This is very important for your company's success. Look at it this way: If your plan is based on hoping that your team will adapt to your learning style, ask yourself this: Is constantly retraining or reshuffling staff in your company's budget?

Everyone, of course, has some combination of Audio, Visual, and Kinetic learning ability. One of the great examples of AVK is a yoga class. The teacher calls out the instructions in audio, demonstrates the movement for visual, and the student tries the position as kinetic.

What's your learning style? If you have a tough time when the yoga instructor stops demonstrating, you're probably a visual learner. If the instructor gives a verbal mental image and that works for you, then you favor audio. If you simply have to practice the movement until you get good at it, then you're a kinetic learner.

So when someone asks you to either show them, write it down, or explain it again, it's in your best interest to honor that request. Hear *their* Learning DRUMBEAT.

INTERLEAVING

The concept of interleaving has come to the fore in the recent controversy over education reform and teaching-to-the-test. This is the opposite. It's the moment between amateur and maestro. You can achieve true mastery when you come at a subject from different vantage points or contexts, and with different learning styles.

There's also mounting evidence that the only true way to mastery is through deep practice. The simplest Beat is to practice what you're bad at (not what you're already good at). Once you aren't bad at something anymore, your new knowledge and ability get chunked into the rest of what you're already good at, and you get even better.

In *Mindshift: Break Through Obstacles to Learning and Discover Your Hidden Potential*, author Barbara Oakley refers to the two different states of mind as either focus or diffuse. You can't have both at the same time.

We'll revisit this concept again in the Innovation Drum and Teamwork Drum chapters, but especially of interest is that the two types of thinkers have different strengths and weaknesses. "Race car thinkers" are frequently the first to find a solution, but they often miss the details that "Hiker thinkers" see along the way. To become a DRUMBEAT Thinker, you need to understand the difference—and set the appropriate pace for YOUR House of Thinking.

When writing this book, I used many different pathways to organize the material, including mind maps, questions, articles, books, test paragraphs, outlining, more outlining, combinatory play, real life applications in one to ones, pre-planning meetings, role-playing dialogue in my head, and more outlining. The interleaving effect was fantastic. Each method informs the others.

WHAT'S THE GOAL OF ALL THIS CONTINUOUS LEARNING?

The goal of continuous learning is continuous improvement. The Japanese word for this is Kaizen. The Kaizen process has four parts: Plan, Do, Check, and Act.

Let's look at operating a piece of equipment as an example. In order to avoid a frequent mistake, the current best practice can be illustrated with words and pictures on a laminated card that hangs next to the machine.

In sales, the Kaizen process could include working through the best answers to all the possible objections a prospect could possibly muster. If the sales team encounters or thinks of a new objection, then a new Kaizen card is added to each sales station.

THREE SIMPLE LEARNING STRATEGIES

1. Block a 30-minute Finales! Sessions to read articles, watch a video, or listen to an audio chapter. One of the only times multitasking actually works is when you can listen to an audio book while driving, on the treadmill, or doing chores. This is especially effective for kinetic learners: If you want a really clean house, listen to a great audio book while you're tidying up.

2. There are many free classes online as well. You might play backup band to your strengths and choose a course on something totally new. Or get some practice time in on a weakness.

3. After each class, video, or session make note of what you found most interesting. Consider writing a concise five-sentence paragraph using the BRIEF method from the book *Brief: Make a Bigger Impact by Saying Less* by Joseph McCormack. Put it in a Learning Journal, or if it's got a good potential use, throw it in the bottom of your Kettle Drum to review at a later date. Even better, if you blog,

keep it in a folio of idea "packets" to draw upon when you're coming up dry for content. My definition of packets is more than a paragraph, less than a page.

\

CHAPTER REVIEW

The first Skill Drum is to learn, so that you know what you're talking about. There are phases to learning, which flow from unconsciously incompetent to consciously incompetent, to consciously competent, to unconsciously competent. We are all at different phases on different topics. It's important to understand that people learn in different ways, including audio, visual, kinetic, and in combination; an interleaving of all three is often the most powerful. The goal is not to let any institutional knowledge get away from the company. Use processes like Kaizen to memorialize the best routines and habits. If you and your company are a learning organization, you all will make fewer mistakes, have happier customers, and enjoy a healthier culture.

\|

THREE BEATS TO REMEMBER

\ Everyone has something to learn. Start with what's most important.

| Experiment with the learning style(s) that work best for you.

/ Always share important learning with others in a permanent way.

\|/

PRACTICE

Individuals

To practice audio learning, listen to an audio book on an interesting topic. To practice visual learning, try watching a TED talk once a week at the same time to establish a habit. To practice kinetic learning, mock up a Kaizen card on something you learned. It doesn't have to be professional-looking; it just has to clearly state the process.

Teams/Band of Characters

Watch a TED talk together once a week and schedule time to discuss it afterward. How might it be applied to your department?

Large companies

Strive to have a full Kaizen for every job position. Make it available to new hires earlier rather than later.
\|//

LEARNING NOTES

Keep track of interesting things to learn about here.

What are your next four learning beats going to be?

1	2	3	4

CHAPTER 8

// Innovation Drum

THE NEXT BE-ING SKILL DRUM DEFIES LOGIC. It can't be found when you're searching for it, but stop looking . . . and it appears. It can't really be put on a schedule, but schedule time to "not" look for it anyway. And when this drum appears, you better get some Beats in while you can.

What's the name of this Skill? It's the Innovation Drum. Creativity and muse help answer its question, "What's possible?"

Throughout most of my career, Innovation has been my default drum. If the solution to a problem seemed lacking, how might we find a better one? The answer lies in knowing where not to look.

COMBINATORY PLAY

Like in John Sebastian's song "Do You Believe in Magic?" sometimes thinking outside the box resembles magic but there are some processes that help move things along. The first one is combinatory play. While most analytical problems are best solved on neat and orderly desks, creative problems are best solved with an office that more resembles a cartoon.

Call it the mess on the desk, or an offal office. A fusion of colors, sounds, shapes, and improbable combinations all help us make new and unique neural connections. Eat different foods with different smells during an Innovation Session. Sit in a different seat, or don't sit at all. Listen to new music to get you in the mood. Play with toys or oddities. Give your subconscious something to talk about.

All of these improbable combinations help us see things in a different way. I've seen solutions for the restaurant industry work at a realty firm. Perhaps a subscription model could be adapted for your industry. What can you do that no one else will? How can you do something better than everyone else? What would Einstein do? WWED.

> "WE CAN'T SOLVE PROBLEMS BY USING THE SAME KIND OF THINKING WE USED WHEN WE CREATED THEM."
> —*Albert Einstein*

DELAY CONVERGENT THINKING

There are two kinds of thinking in problem-solving: divergent and convergent. For innovation work, it's really important to delay converging on solutions too early in the process. We are hard-wired to solve problems quickly and move on. It's called a bias to action, and it's the innovation killer.

If you do a Porter's Five Forces review, AirBnB had almost no threat of new entrants because it was the new entrant.

There was no threat of substitution because it itself was the substitution for hotels. Its pricing power was distributed locally in the marketplace. Its input costs were very low. And its current competition was already booked full—so it actually served as a post-competition sale. It yielded a perfect five star industry (if not necessarily five star rooms).

In 1990, I was literally one decision away from having the AirBnB business model. (More on that story in the next chapter.)

It was my convergent thinking—based on assumptions about not being complicit in breaking the law—which kept us from one outrageously innovative solution for frustrated travelers. The mistakes are almost always in the assumptions. What assumptions have you converged upon too quickly in your department or business? To find out, try out the exercises offered at the end of this chapter. There is controversy around innovation methods so try a few and see which deliver the best results for you.

If you're unaccustomed to these innovation parts, there's a process you might like called 100:10:1 by Nick Bentley. In Bentley's model, you don't allow anyone to discuss answers until they have put 100 possible solutions on the table. Then start converging by whittling that 100 down to 10 via discussion and/or ballot voting. Finally, decide on one.

The 100:10:1 process resembles brainstorming, which is getting a bad rap these days as a decision-making process. As mentioned earlier in this book, Dr. Tony McCaffery has a method called Brainswarming, which is a productivity upgrade. It combines the top-down thinking of the former, but adds a bottom-up approach that utilizes resources.

In defense of brainstorming, Stuart Brown's book *Play: How it Shapes the Brain, Opens the Imagination, and Invigorates the Soul* suggests that fun is the missing ingredient for a successful session. Without fun, brainstorming is just thinly veiled office politics. When it's a game and done with a certain affection for the topic different parts of the brain are accessed. It's here that creative breakthroughs can be made.

When vision, strategy, and resources converge, there is usually a very innovative answer that is based on both process and practicality, or do-ability. You might think of Brainswarming as what might happen if Albert Einstein and the fictional TV character MacGyver, who could repurpose almost any physical object, had a 60-minute Jam session with a whiteboard.

A FOUR-SQUARE APPROACH

In G. Michael Maddock, Luisa C. Uriarte, and Paul B. Brown's book *Brand New: Solving the Innovation Paradox*, they offer a tool for budgeting innovation Sets, Sessions, and days. They propose a four-square with Customer Knows or Doesn't Know What They Want on one axis, and is it Easy or Difficult to Provide on the other axis.

The names of the quadrants are Fast Fail/Succeed if Known and Easy; Evolutionary if Known and Difficult; Revolutionary if Doesn't Know and Difficult; and Differentiation if Doesn't Know but Easy. The aha moment for me was that you can budget your available innovation time in these quadrants based on your strategic plan. Adjust as necessary.

SPEAK LAST

Here's a tip to help you stop converging too quickly. When holding your meetings, let everyone else speak before you do. After you name the topic, or set a goal for the meeting, you speak last. Let all your Band of Characters participate in the divergence portion of the meeting, first. If you speak before then, whatever you say will almost always start a convergence on what the boss really wants.

Why is speaking last a best practice? You get to hear everyone else's input first. See your team interact. Who has a unique insight, maybe even the best answer? This allows you more time to think about errors, omissions, and creative solutions.

If you have a different idea to offer when it's finally your turn, you're the superstar. If, on the other hand, it's all been said, you haven't risked any social capital being called a micromanager. Rather, you're the superstar for letting the team shine. Either way it's a Win Storm.

This quote captures the essence of DRUMBEAT Leadership.

"I THINK THE DRUMMER SHOULD SIT BACK THERE AND PLAY SOME DRUMS, AND NEVER MIND ABOUT THE TUNES. JUST GET UP THERE AND WAIL BEHIND WHOEVER IS SITTING UP THERE PLAYING THE SOLO. AND THIS IS WHAT IS LACKING, DEFINITELY LACKING IN MUSIC TODAY."

—*Buddy Rich*

Group Facilitation

Group process is tricky. While someone on the team tries to run the meeting, it's really difficult or impossible to likewise participate. Also, the person running the meeting is setting themselves up as above the rest of the team. Every company I've ever worked with is amazed how great their first professionally facilitated meeting went. If your company can't afford to pay for meeting facilitation, you might consider borrowing a team member with those skills from a noncompeting neighbor, and then returning the favor. Also, I've seen local educators do this as a side hustle. Be a BIG fan of small tests, treat your team to a facilitated meeting, and you just might find it more than pays for itself in productivity gains.

DAY-TO-DAY WELL BEING

The last Beat for the Innovation Drum is based on a study entitled "Creative Activities Promote Day-to-Day Wellbeing" by Dr. Tamlin Connor at The University of Ocala in New Zealand.

According to the study, daily creative tapping on our Innovation Drum has the added benefit of a "wellness hangover" the next day: a feel-good dividend. Personally, I attribute it to being deeply in touch with your creative self. Why wouldn't you want to hang out a little bit with that cool cat everyday? You can, if you make innovation part of your DRUMBEAT.

DIVERSITY

Innovation teams thrive on diversity as well. Get input from different departments, newbies, veterans, people who've worked together successfully before, and successful people who haven't, artists and engineers, younger and older, men and women . . . heck, ask a kid what they think.

There are two types of innovation. A capital "I" Innovation and a small "i" innovation. The former is more on the level of the whole business or major product lines, while the latter is more about smaller improvements in processes and procedures. Every drum in the DRUMBEAT Framework could use a little innovation.

"THE THREE THINGS THAT MOTIVATE CREATIVE PEOPLE—
AUTONOMY, MASTERY, PURPOSE!"

—*Daniel Pink*

WARNING

If management never rewards innovative thinking, and instead always does the same old same old, your company will fall behind. Remember, your competition is playing with its processes, procedures, and product lines for continual improvement.
\

CHAPTER REVIEW

The Innovation Drum is very different than all the other drums in terms of processes, meetings, and attitude. Because of rapid iterations in all areas of business today, companies need to exercise their innovation muscles differently than other skills. Time should regularly be budgeted for Sessions to work on projects with varying timelines and urgencies. Innovations can be large and small, and they can spill over into other drums and teams in the company. Management needs to be aware that it is all too easy to kill innovation in their culture by saying "no" too often, taking credit, or over-fiddling with their team's recommendations.

\\

THREE BEATS TO REMEMBER

\ You cannot manage innovation like other drums.

| While you can schedule Innovation Sessions, it's more like jamming for new riffs.

/ Diverse teams, divergent thinking, and combinatory play are keys.

\|/

PRACTICE

Individuals

Wander for Inspiration: Next time you're stuck on a challenge or opportunity that's begging for an innovative approach, go to a mall, a museum, or a gallery and just wander around. You may trigger a new way to solve that puzzle.

Teams/Band of Characters

Question Mark Exercise: Have everyone on your team—including you—write down as many assumptions about your business as you can. Then change the periods to question marks. Typically an innovation will emerge out of seeing these assumptions in question form, and realizing that the assumption is incorrect.

LARGE COMPANIES

Invest in Be-ability: You've probably heard of do-ability, but have you ever heard of BE-ability? If you have a place at your company to set up a "creative" space for innovation work, consider stocking it with all manner of artistic supplies, images, sounds, and smells. It might just be the best investment you'll ever make.

\|//

INNOVATION DRUM NOTES

Next time you need to get out of your head to do some thinking, try coloring. Here's a Drumkit to practice on.

MINDMAP

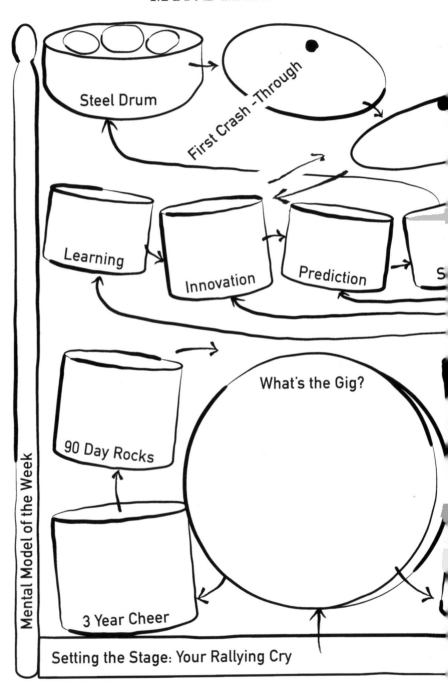

Steel Drum

First Crash-Through

Learning

Innovation

Prediction

S

90 Day Rocks

What's the Gig?

3 Year Cheer

Mental Model of the Week

Setting the Stage: Your Rallying Cry

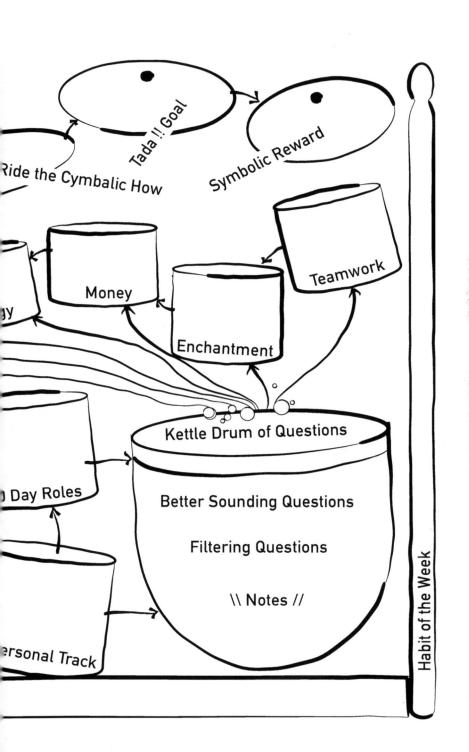

INNOVATION DRUM NOTES

What are three areas that would benefit from some small "i" innovation and some capital "I" Innovation?

CHAPTER 9

// Prediction Drum

THERE'S A FAMOUS SAYING: "The map is not the territory."

The point is that no matter how many different routes can take you to your destination, you won't know which to take until you actually hit the road. You might not even know whether your route plan was accurate and up to date until you see the reality of the terrain you're covering.

In other words, you need to pound the Forecasting Drum to know where you are in the business cycle and how you stand in your industry. It's the only way to have a good grip on the best assumptions to start beating the Strategy Drum in the next chapter.

The Forecasting Drum provides the beauty of knowing what Beat you should be-doing because it will move your market.

One of the challenges that face most of us is that we tend to be a lot more rational than the behaviors we're trying to predict. In *Predictably Irrational: The Hidden Forces That Shape Our Decisions*, behavioral economist Dan Ariely makes the point that habits, rather than logic, rule most of our day.

"EVEN THE MOST ANALYTICAL THINKERS ARE PREDICTABLY IRRATIONAL; THE REALLY SMART ONES ACKNOWLEDGE AND ADDRESS THEIR IRRATIONALITIES."

— Dan Ariely

Humans can only handle deep, conscious, highest quality thinking for about three hours per day. In business, this can translate into all of our rational efforts being pitted against consumers' bad habits of not buying our products or services.

Our brains are wired to stick with habitual mental maps. It's a good idea to have your Band of Characters challenge these maps. Having regular Prediction Drum meetings is very helpful in maintaining a good idea of what's ahead for your company.

A detailed infographic called the Codex of Cognitive Biases is often seen in poster form. It displays hundreds of specific thinking behaviors that most people exhibit. (One of these cognitive biases is that "We favor the immediate, relatable thing in front of us.") Reading through these, you begin to wonder about the whole "free will" thing. Either way, it shows us that it's probably time to spend a little more quality time with our Chief Thinking Officers.

HOW TO MAKE MORE ACCURATE PREDICTIONS

The importance of the Prediction Drum is to make decisions based on the best assumptions possible—but not take too much time doing it. Let's look at the extremes of the decision-making scale. Paralysis by analysis is a real problem, and it's very common. On the other hand, big data analysis does solve many problems that no one could have possibly imagined. Traffic data derived by the speed that cell phones are traveling? Genius!

So how do we find our DRUMBEAT between the two extremes? The quality of your business predictions matters a lot—but some of the most spectacularly bad decisions are made because of errors in an assumption. That's why you need a highly structured process to review assumptions, forecasts, and the path.

Here are some suggestions for your Prediction Drum process, starting with macro and working our way to micro.

MACRO PREDICTIONS: BANGING ON A CRYSTAL DRUM

On the most macro level, Kevin Kelly's book, *Inevitable: Understanding the Twelve Technological Forces That Will Shape Our Future*, looks into the crystal ball to predict the future of a wide range of goods and services.

In *Bowling with a Crystal Ball: How to predict technology trends, create disruptive implementations and navigate them through industry*, author Yoram Soloman suggests we use a process that takes the most recent advances in technology in one sector and try to apply them to another industry. As an Innovation strategy, you might try practicing on a different industry from yours first, because it's easier to give advice to others than to yourself. If you come up with an insight, it probably can also be applied to your business.

Remember, your competitors have access to these tools too. Sometimes whoever gets there first wins.

Where are you in the business cycle? You are either approaching a peak in business activity, just past the peak and on your way down, near the bottom, or just past bottom on the upswing. Acknowledging your current (and forecasted) position is crucial to making wise business decisions.

For example, if you know you're approaching—or just past—the peak, it might be a good idea to conserve some cash, maybe sell an asset you don't really need when demand is high, or be a little less patient with significantly underperforming team members.

If you are approaching the bottom, or you just passed a trough, it might be a good idea to use some cash to buy assets on sale from those who forgot to plan. You might also start looking to hire some A players who, through no fault of their own, may be looking for work.

You can learn more about the microeconomics of the business cycle in the book *Make Your Move: Change the Way You Look At Your Business and Increase Your Bottom Line* by Alan N. Beaulieu and Brian L. Beaulieu.

MICRO PREDICTIONS

Zeroing in closer, how is your specific industry and business doing? Where can you get reliable data? Are you underperforming or outperforming your competition? How aggressive do you need to get to compete?

We previously looked at Porter's Five Forces. If you are mostly in a positive industry (meaning there is little chance of new entrants, no imminent threat of substitution, stable or dropping input costs, stable pricing or potential for increases, and you're currently gaining more than your fair market share) then you can be a little sloppy. Little mistakes probably won't matter much. What matters, however, is speed. This is the time to grab market share!

If you are mostly in a negative industry (meaning there is a strong chance of new entrants, a substitution for your product or service on the horizon, input cost pressures, a price war, and you aren't getting your fair market share), then you need to seriously up your game. Being sloppy about not using best practices in your Strategy Drum will likely put you out of business.

What should you be predicting? Predictions fall into two categories, financial and managerial. Assuming you already understand the importance and use of budgets, actual vs. forecasts, year over year, moving averages, etc., be sure you also know how to measure the performance of your company's management and team members.

A method used at Intel is called Objectives and Key Results (OKR). This lets you measure and therefore predict not only financial goals but behavioral ones. There is definitely a style issue here to discuss. I've read passionate white papers which argue that sticking to the Money Drum numbers is the best strategy.

I've also read very convincing sales arguments stating that if you know you're going to close 1 in 10 leads, and you want 10 sales, you simply have to pitch 100 times. In other words, manage the number of pitches and the financial results will follow. This falls more under the Teamwork Drum.

But no matter where your style falls in this debate, one thing is certain: If you can forecast it, you can plan for it. And planning gives you time to react. For example, if your close ratio is up, investigate the bright spots, share, iterate, and adjust your financial forecasts.

If your close ratio is down, check to see if it is a personnel execution problem . . . or maybe your processes or training practices need a tune up. As long as you've already carried out quality macro forecasting, and eliminated any bad assumptions, you can be reasonably confident that you're having a management issue.

You'll have a much stronger Beat after you master the Forecasting Drum. Don't neglect this drum, or you will certainly have bad days in your future. When things aren't going well, it's the first drum to check. The most spectacular mistakes happen because of bad assumptions and you won't get good forecasts unless you know what to measure and how often.

BEWARE MEAN REVERSION

I've seen many a panicked executive start drawing conclusions from bad data or a statistical anomaly simply because they don't understand mean reversion. Let's say you have an unexpectedly bad month or quarter. But nothing in your models shows any red flags. In baseball, a .250 hitter doesn't always get a hit every 4 times at bat. There will be times they often get on base, and other times it can take a lot more than four at bats to get a hit. At the end of the season a .250 batter is usually really close to .250. This is called reversion to the mean.

One forecasting tool around this is a 12-month moving average. This will smooth out the irregularities in your numbers. Don't get me wrong; bad numbers are still a yellow light and cause for concern. But they're not necessarily reason to panic.

\

CHAPTER REVIEW

Many businesses don't have any system for forecasting properly. This can cause needless anxiety and a really poor DRUMBEAT. A robust system looks at macro trends all the way down to micro matters. It's critical to know if you are underperforming or outperforming your industry, and how healthy or challenged it is. Good forecasting lets you set routines for your teams to follow so there's a healthy and steady DRUMBEAT. Planning at least a quarter out will help your company rock and roll with the best of them!

\|

THREE BEATS TO REMEMBER

\   How healthy is your industry and where are you in the business cycle?

| Are you underperforming or outperforming your industry?

/   What routine changes will you follow if your results differ from forecast?

\|/

PRACTICE

Individuals

Set up a rolling twelve-month analysis of your key metric. How are you really doing?

Teams/Band of Characters

What routines will you follow on a weekly basis if actual results differ from forecast?

Large companies

What strategic moves should you be making right now based on where you think you are in the business cycle? Can you get confirmation that your forecasting is sound?

\|//

FORECASTING DRUM NOTES

What were your four most important takeaways from this chapter for your industry?

FORECASTING DRUM NOTES

What were your four most important takeaways from this chapter for your company?

CHAPTER 10

// Strategy Drum

To STRATEGIZE EFFECTIVELY, the question "What should we do?" (or the BSQ, "How are we going to win?") must be answered—and it must be answered within the context of a longer timeframe.

To do this, the Learning, Innovation, and Prediction Drums must give way to the Strategy Drum, which also covers money, enchantment, and teamwork. These areas must be addressed within the context of a longer timeframe. And where the Learning, Innovation, and Prediction Drums are based more on the art of figuring out what to do, the Strategy Drum leverages both art and science about equally.

Here's the rub: How do you define "winning"? In a football game or a war, what constitutes a "win" is pretty obvious. In business, however, it might mean anything from surviving a business cycle, to getting a minimally viable product, to not becoming obsolete, to providing jobs, to earning a certain amount of money, to grabbing local market share, to being the country leader, to conquering the world, or even to gaining the ability to simply sell it and cash out.

Goals and Strategy are like a two-Beat rhythm. Goals are played on the bass drums, and the Strategy Drum is central. Goals are the minimum results you hope to get. Strategy is how you're going to achieve those results. Goals are quantifiably measurable. Strategy measurement is almost impossible, or very tricky at best.

If this sounds a bit squishy, you have a good ear. At the time of this writing, a search for "Strategy" on Amazon yielded over 200,000 results, and on Google, 690 million. It's obviously not a subject on which there is consensus.

When it comes to strategizing, the CEO may be working too little, just enough, or too much. She may be unhappy, content, or thrilled about any of these conditions. And if it's too chaotic for the leader to set goals and a strategies, what does it feel like for the team when they don't have any say in these Beats?

The Strategy Drum is central in the DRUMBEAT framework. In fact, it's smack dab in the middle on the one-page mind map. So how do you align the CEO or owner's DRUMBEAT with the team's when it comes to the Strategy Drum?

Here's a default Strategy to get you started. Adjust as needed.

THE TWO-BEAT WINNING RHYTHM

First BEAT

State your winning strategy in the simplest terms.

Are you going to win by:

- Having the best service in the industry?
- Having the most durable products?
- Having the best selection?
- Being the only reliable source?
- Being the best neighbor?
- Being there when needed every time?
- Something else?

What's your competitive advantage?

Second BEAT Default

Winning is making sure the customer is delighted, the team is thriving, profits are acceptable or better, the business plan appears safe in a three-year timeframe, you challenge the plan regularly, and you're having fun.

STRATEGY DRUM CONUNDRUM: HOW TO DECIDE?

Some folks believe that winning is making tons of great small decisions every day. Others believe that people are successful as a result of making one spectacularly good decision. So how do you determine which path to follow?

This will help you make better decisions, faster. Kahneman (and others) suggest keeping a decision journal to track each decision to see how you're do-ing. This can be reviewed, perhaps on a DRUMBEAT of every rock or quarter.

Here's how to score your decisions: You either made a good or bad decision, and you either reached a good or bad outcome. Farnam Street's Re:Think Decisions Four-Square gives a little more depth to these scores:

Good outcome, good process: Success and maybe some luck too.

Good outcome, bad process: Gambling with pathological optimism.

Bad outcome, bad process: Gambling, then blaming others for losses.

Bad outcome, good process: A loss due to bad luck, so don't kill the process!

What decisions are journal-worthy? Set a minimum dollar limit, and anything having to do with a core belief or assumption about your industry, business, or customers. Remember that while you are doing your best to be rational, you can't count on your audience and customers to be equally rational. And while the Strategy doesn't always have to be rational, it does have to get you to the goal.

Studies have shown that we are far more motivated by fear of loss than hope of gain. In other words, we default to less risk. That might be good or bad.

MINDSET

One of the first things to consider before pounding the Strategy Drum is your state of mind. In *Mindset: The New Psychology of Success*, author Carol Dweck tells a story about a successful baker who one day sees a new bakery being built across the street.

The first baker has a couple of choices: He can start a price war if his mindset states that there is not enough business in town to support two bakeries. He could alternately make sure that the quality of his baked goods and service keeps his customer experience compelling. He could even look at the possibilities that are revealed when two great bakeries actually increase the demand for baked goods overall.

The former is a scarcity mindset; the latter, an abundance mindset. Neither is better or worse. Granted, small- and medium-sized businesses have a much more difficult time if they choose to compete on price, as larger companies will always have a competitive advantage due to economies of scale. But the point is that you can't pound the Strategy Drum until you resolve your mindset.

STAY CURRENT

Business is moving so fast that your great decisions today may need updating and multiple iterations even tomorrow. You may need to respond to an innovation thrown down by a competitor. Your entire industry might swing from Porter's Five Forces positive to negative. In these and many other cases, you'll have to change your strategy.

Again, Goals are not a Strategy, and Strategy is not the goal. If you're a golfer, the goal is par. But your challenge may be to arc around some trees—and your strategy is to play the hook. Whether you execute the hook properly doesn't mean the strategy was good or bad, but your swing is. Your swing is in the execution (the Money Drum, coming in the next chapter).

Goals, then Strategy, then New Goals, then . . . AirBnB's initial Goal was to help desperate business travelers. The Strategy was to match these travelers with unused residential space online. At the time AirBnB launched, Porter's Five Forces were probably 5 star positive, meaning they could make a ton of mistakes and still be successful.

AirBnB's results blew way past the goal of a successful business: It is now the largest lodging operation in the world—and it owns no rooms. Before AirBnB existed, I was the CEO of a hotel chain that was one decision away from the AirBnB strategy, twenty years prior.

We had a reservation system for over 500 Bed and Breakfasts. Many B&Bs were little more than a couple spare bedrooms in someone's home. We did our best to make sure they were all legally licensed and zoned correctly.

We were literally and figuratively one reservation away from making the transition from small B&Bs to residential rooms: We hesitated to delve into the myriad regulations of licensing across the country.

See how Strategy can miss being spectacular by one small variable?

A STRATEGY-STRATEGY: BIG UPSIDE, LITTLE DOWNSIDE

The wisest investors only take deals when a strategy has a defined, minimal risk and an astounding potential upside. Note that this has nothing to do with the state of the industry, dreams, society, family, friendship, or anything else.

Now, if you want to include other items (besides getting to or blowing past an objective with minimum risk), you absolutely can do that. We'll discuss that in Chapter 18. This is a style issue, and obviously style isn't strategy. Strategy is putting into place processes for making spectacularly good decisions (and/or lots of little decisions) that will achieve your goal.

Let's use the example of musicians considering risking the financial expense of a studio Session. The strategy may be to spend a week in your garage with three or four of your buds, a few lyrics, a couple of riffs . . . and see what happens.

Or you can throw together some of the best musicians in the world, grab a studio for a weekend, and pretty much know what'll happen. That's precisely the strategy behind the Traveling Wilburys. George Harrison, Bob Dylan, Tom Petty, and Jeff Lynne knew they needed the insurance of adding a "voice" to be successful. So they strategically invited legend Roy Orbison to be that voice.

Would they have been a breakout without Orbison's haunting vocals? We'll never know. But their risk of failure went way down, and their chance for success went way up when Orbison agreed.

THAT'S HOW YOU POUND THE STRATEGY DRUM. If you do the best you can with a great strategy, the odds of success go way up. In fact, with a great strategy you can even fall short of your best effort, and still win.

I know several folks who sold all their stocks at the bottom of the market in 2009 because they were scared. Those who didn't do anything, on the other hand, have been richly rewarded for their sloth. Doing nothing in this situation was a fabulous strategy. The sellers, in retrospect, were overly risk averse.

What's your risk/reward tolerance? It's difficult to pound the Strategy Drum without knowing. Much has been written about emotions vs. logic in decision making. Warren Buffet, for example, says investors need to be greedy when others are terrified, and terrified when others are greedy. With success like his, it's difficult to argue his strategy.

TIME TO DECIDE!

When putting words to music, knowing when to say "yes" and when to say "no" is a major part of your personal DRUMBEAT. This requires you to make a decision. How good are you at making decisions?

Kahneman focuses on the spectacularly good decision. Yale political scientist Hélène Landemore has demonstrated that people who make good decisions 49% of the time are on a downward spiral—while those who are only 2% better (51% good decisions) are on an upward spiral.

How might we go about measuring good and bad decisions? We've already talked about keeping a decision journal for yourself. How about one for each of your Band of Characters for review? Much the way Filtering Questions work in your Kettle, keeping score of your decision-making processes will really help you to be supremely productive.

SIX THINKING HATS

Design your own decision page. Here is a sample default system that you can use as a starting point. We'll take a closer look at these Six Thinking Hats in Chapter 13.

1. State the decision that has to be made as clearly as possible: How might we/I decide . . . ?

2. What are the facts? (White Hat Thinking)

3. How do you feel about it? (Red Hat Thinking)

4. What do you want? (Yellow Hat Thinking)

5. What are the risks? (Black Hat Thinking)

6. Let's get creative. (Green Hat Thinking)

7. What are the next steps to make this decision? (Blue Hat Thinking)

WRAP

Another process is called WRAP. In *Decisive: How to Make Better Choices in Work and Life*, authors Chip Heath & Dan Heath identify the four ailments of decision making as Narrow Framing, Confirmation Bias, Short Term Emotion, and Over-Confidence. The prescription is called WRAP, which stands for

Widen your options,
Reality-test your assumptions,
Attain distance before deciding, and
Prepare to be wrong.

Here's another reason to make sure you have a formal decision-making process. I bet you have the chops to support both sides of an argument and be totally persuasive. I would also bet that members in your Band of Characters could do the same. Anyone with any talent in financial analysis can find data to support their position. So how are you supposed to make a spectacularly good decision? McKinsey & Co. has published that process beats analysis by a factor of six. You'll save a lot of useless arguing, too.

VETTING

So, you've finally arrived at a great Strategy. You're all fired up. You used your process. Your confidence is high. Now what?

Time to get some unbiased feedback. The challenge is to be sure it's unbiased. Someone who loves you may not want to discourage you, or may want to spare your feelings. (Not a good feedback source.) Consultants earn more the longer the clock runs, so their bias may be indecision.

Here are two better ways to go: One is to join a peer group from noncompeting businesses. The whole point of joining is to help each other succeed by making better decisions, faster. In the boards I facilitate, there is care and trust—but we challenge each other to grow. Think of this as the Kettle, but with really successful people helping you filter the Strategies. You can read more about private advisory boards in *The Power of Peers: How the Company You Keep Drives Leadership, Growth, and Success* by Leon Shapiro and Leo Bottary.

The second is to set up a Red Team. In the armed forces, a Red Team is charged with finding the holes in your strategy. The point is this: After the Red Team is finished, you're either more confident, better informed and ready with new contingents, or you're ready to abandon the strategy.

No matter which of these two you use to vet a strategy, you won't be accused of being a compulsive gambler.

The Red Team helps you play better defense and offense. But what if there isn't any competition at all? That would be a Blue Ocean Strategy from a book by the same name by W. Chan Kim and Renee Mauborgne, *Blue Ocean Strategy: How to Create Uncontested Market Space and Make the Competition Irrelevant*. When AirBnB first launched, they were essentially the only peer-to-peer room renting service. There were no other "boats" competing; they had clear blue ocean all to themselves. If you can find a new way of doing something, or you can do something no one else can do, happy sailing. It could be a wonderful ride.

FINAL NOTE

The Strategy Drum has a head game attached to it that the other drums don't. I call it the Ambivalence Plateau.

Let's say your department or business or industry is doing fine. You're doing fine. The family is doing fine. It's all good. If you start whaling on the Strategy Drum, things are going to have to start changing—and change isn't easy. The plateau of ambivalence can stop good businesses from becoming great. But bear in mind that if you thought of it, someone else probably will think of it too—and soon. You can get out ahead or play catch-up. It depends on how you roll.
\

CHAPTER REVIEW

Have a goal and a process to set a Strategy, and vet the Strategy with trusted peers. At the end of the day, answering, "What should we do?" is on you. Without a process, you're pretty much just gambling. As in the gaming industry, the house always wins because they have a process; they're not gambling. If you don't have a winning strategy, the rest of the industry, your competitors, are indeed "the house." What's your strategic process? How are you going to win?

\|

THREE BEATS TO REMEMBER

\ Strategy is how you are going to win to achieve your goal.

| Having a process to decide on a Strategy prevents gambling.

/ Once you have a Strategy, vet it with peers or a Red Team.

\|/

PRACTICE

Individuals

Write up a formal procedure to follow to make important decisions. Consider things like always sleeping on an important decision before implementation. If everyone agrees too quickly, is it a good decision, or groupthink? Are you missing an important aspect? Is your strategy understandable to an entry-level person in the organization?

Teams/Band of Characters

In your decision-making process you'll need to pound on the Innovation Drum to make sure you aren't missing some spectacularly good idea. Innovation meetings aren't run the same way as staff meetings. Build in some dedicated Innovation drumming with your Band of Characters before settling into your strategy.

Large companies

Encourage the use of decision journals for your teams. Review any losses and decide if these were due to the process involved, or simply due to a lack of luck. Adjust the process as necessary. You need losses to improve your process. Treasure what you can measure . . . and consider keeping a personal score on your decisions and those of your teams.

\|//

Strategy Drum Notes

How are you going to win for each product or service line?

Strategy Drum Notes

What makes you NOT a commodity?

CONVERGING WITH THE DO-ING SNARES

Once the Strategy is set, it's time to get it all done—playing your three Do-ing Snare Drums: Money, Enchantment, and Teamwork.

Playing the Enchantment Drum, you inspire your clients and your audience to support your product or service. This is the most important activity your business can do today.

Keep everyone in the loop by playing your Teamwork Drum, because nothing can get done if your players aren't supported.

Before those, however, you must start by beating on your Money Drum. This is where you execute your strategy. Let's take a closer look at this drum.

CHAPTER 11

// Money Drum

"SOMETIMES I AM TWO PEOPLE. JOHNNY IS THE NICE ONE.
CASH CAUSES ALL THE TROUBLE. THEY FIGHT."
— *Johnny Cash*

THE MONEY DRUM IS ABOUT EXECUTING YOUR STRATEGY.
The trick is in doing so while balancing your goals with the
needs of your Team.

HOW TO SET SMART GOALS

First, take all the great work you've done in goal setting, and
break up your strategy into smaller, achievable parts. Charles
Doran is credited with a process known as SMART Goals:
Be Specific, create Measurable goals, get Agreement, and
determine who is Responsible by a set Time.

There is a bit of controversy about individual SMART
goals versus team SMART goals. Some pundits proclaim

that only individual team members should have their own goals; otherwise time will be wasted playing the blame game. Other gurus state that individual goals foster a culture of individuals, which, although quite common, is not an optimal way to do business.

David Logan and John King's book *Tribal Leadership: Leveraging Natural Groups to Build a Thriving Organization*, gives five ways to describe your tribe. These are: "Life Sucks," "My Life Sucks," "I'm Great," "We're Great," and "Life's Great."

If your organization is made up primarily of individuals who are out for themselves, then your company may be stuck in the cultural middle. If that is acceptable to you, fine. But if your strategy needs teamwork then you've got some DRUMBEAT thinking to do.

You personally may be doing a great job. But how about your Trio, Band of Characters, and the rest of the company you keep? How can you help your team be more successful?

> "...IT TURNS OUT THAT TRIBES, NOT MONEY, NOT FACTORIES, THAT CAN CHANGE OUR WORLD, THAT CAN CHANGE POLITICS, THAT CAN ALIGN LARGE NUMBERS OF PEOPLE. NOT BECAUSE YOU FORCE THEM TO DO SOMETHING AGAINST THEIR WILL. BUT BECAUSE THEY WANTED TO CONNECT."
> —*Seth Godin*

BETTER: SMART-EST GOALS

What's a great drummer to do? Make sure to have both individual and team SMART goals. Even better, try having

SMART-EST goals—with the EST for Enthusiastically-run Small Tests on Better Sounding SMART Goals. The DRUMBEAT above all else is about thinking, which is highly underrated.

In *The 4 Disciplines of Execution: Achieving Your Wildly Important Goals*, authors McChesney, Covey, and Huling recommend an exercise for setting SMART goals:

Pick a verb, like "increase." Pick a lagging measure, like revenue growth. Pick a deliverable, like 20%. Last, pick a deadline, like "the end of the quarter." The SMART goal is then: "Increase revenue growth by 20% by quarter's end."

Now, break it down into parts, based on what each department, team, Band of Characters, and individual need to do in order to get there.

This raises another question. Some experts claim that the outcome to manage is simply the goal. Other consultants have a construct to manage the behaviors that, if practiced, will achieve the goal. The former simply wants each individual to increase sales by at least 20% or else. The latter knows that if you close 1 out of 10 pitches, you'll need to pitch about 20% more clients for a 20% increase in revenue, or find a way to increase the close rate from 10 sales to 12 sales out of 100 pitches.

What's the SMARTEST drummer to do? Enthusiastically run Small Tests! Remember Productivity Riff #18: Be a BIG fan of small tests to see what works where and why.

In *SWITCH: How to Change Things When Change is Hard*, Chip and Dan Heath talk about Looking for Bright Spots.

Instead of looking for problems to solve, look for individuals, bands, or teams whose sales are already up 20% and try to iterate those solutions throughout the company. One of the biggest challenges to proper execution is change management, and the book SWITCH is a great place to start.

Now that we have SMART-EST goals, the next step is to keep score of the Beats. Since your goals are measurable, there can be a scoreboard. Remember, "treasure what you measure."

"WE TEND TO OVERVALUE THE THINGS WE CAN MEASURE AND UNDERVALUE THE THINGS WE CANNOT."
—*John Hayes*

Here's the thing about common scoreboards: They can be useful to some team members yet counterproductive to others. Behavioral economics shows that if you fall too far behind the pack, there is a tendency to give up. And giving up isn't the kind of behavior we're trying to instill in our Band of Characters.

Additionally, studies show that the cheerleading necessary to motivate teams is best framed in smallest number terms. In other words, "We're already 10% complete" is more motivational than "We have 90% left to finish." Celebrating the small win of 10% complete tends to motivate members more than focusing on 90% incomplete.

Likewise, "We have only 20% left to go" is preferable to "We're 80% complete." Twenty percent sounds like an easy win. Eighty percent complete sounds like, "heck, we're close enough, don't sweat it." It's important to celebrate small wins together as a team. High fives and fist bumps go a long way to boost morale.

SET UP YOUR SCOREBOARDS

If you're undecided about how to proceed with keeping score in your company, try this: Have teams create a scoreboard and post it in a prominent place. The Team is a team; there is no I in Band or Team.

Likewise, have individuals help create their personal scorecards—but they can keep track of and share their results with the boss on a weekly basis. Additionally, consider having Trios of peers work on their personal scorecards together. (More on Trios in Chapter 17.) It's much easier to work in a small band than in a big group.

Every business is different, so be a BIG fan of small tests and see what works best for you and your company.

Tip: Draw names out of a hat, and divide the your Band of Characters into two teams. Let each team pick a name or a mascot. Make a game out of it, and have some fun. Next month reorganize the teams. After a few months the camaraderie should be palpable. Play your day!

HOW CHALLENGING ARE YOUR GOALS?

Pretend you're Goldilocks, and your goals are the porridge. Should your goals be very challenging? Should they be very easy? Or should they be somewhere in the middle?

I've seen all three approaches work. If the goal appears almost impossible, certain team members often dramatically increase their Beat. On the other hand, I've seen that when easy goals are attained, people get confident enough to stop over-thinking everything—and likewise increase their Beat. Again, be a BIG fan of small tests, see what works, and use it.

BOTTLENECKS, ROADBLOCKS, AND BLOCKHEAD MOVES

As a master drummer, it's your responsibility to be on the lookout for bottlenecks in your processes, and to remove them. The only way to do this is to ask your Band of Characters what's getting in their way. When they tell you, listen. You might need to add team members for certain tasks or steps. You might need to eliminate unnecessary redundancies. Your team may offer an efficiency suggestion. Make it happen!

If they tell you about someone or something that's a roadblock, that's on you to remedy. In the Entrepreneurial Operating System (EOS), from the book *Traction: Get a Grip on Your Business* by Gino Wickman, if you are getting poor performance in an area, it can only be for one of three reasons:

1. You don't have the right person in the right seat, or

2. You didn't train the person properly, or

3. Someone is making too many blockheaded moves and might need to find a new gig.

Notice that two of the three reasons are your responsibility. (Hopefully not all three!)

DON'T MICROMANAGE!

Unlike the boss in Todd Rungren's song "Bang the Drum All Day," your job is to clear obstacles out of your team's way. But it is also your job not to *be* an obstacle. If you can trust your team to reach their goals, then you don't need to micromanage them. If you don't trust them, then trust me—they won't trust you.

Studies have shown that the real reasons people quit their jobs is because the boss is a jerk, and they don't feel empowered to make decisions. For many people, the best way to learn is by making mistakes. This is especially true of kinetic learners. So, try being a good teacher and coach, instead of a micro-manager. You'll probably really like the Beat.

\

CHAPTER REVIEW

The Money Drum is for getting it done. Break your overall strategy into smaller, SMART-EST goals for individuals and for teams. The most difficult part of executing these goals is regularly keeping score of them and holding people accountable. There's an art to deciding whether the goals should be set as easy or difficult. Be a BIG fan of running small tests. When the Money Drum is played correctly, it will give you a really strong Beat.

\|

THREE BEATS TO REMEMBER

\ The Money Drum is about executing your Strategy to achieve your goal.

| Smaller, SMARTEST goals need to be set with the input of your team.

/ Track individual and team scores, and review weekly for accountability.

\|/

PRACTICE

Individuals

Make a list: On the left side, write down all the things you did last week that truly make you look like a jerk with your team. On the right side of the list, write how you might have better handled the situation to have a strong Beat.

Team/Band of Characters

Hold a 60-minute Jam Session to talk about the bottlenecks, roadblocks, and blockheaded moves that are keeping the team from executing your strategy at peak efficiency.

Large companies

Gather all the team's scoreboards to build one overall dashboard for the company. Show the items that are on track in Green, items with an issue in Yellow, and items clearly off track in Red. Start all meetings fixing the Reds. Then discuss the Yellows. You'll never have time to discuss the Greens—but celebrate the Greens while walking around. After all, they're the color of the Money Drum!

\|//

Money Drum Notes

How can you run small tests on attaining BIG performance?

Money Drum Notes

What are your top four ideas?

| 1 | 2 | 3 | 4 |

CHAPTER 12

// Enchantment Drum

THE NEXT DO-ING DRUM, ENCHANTMENT, is where you focus on attracting customers and inspiring them to action. Its question is, "What inspires the audience?" Answering this requires a deep understanding of all the reasons someone would want to buy your product or service.

That's more difficult than it sounds. But once you have settled in on the top few reasons, you can begin telling your company's story. You'll need to refine the messaging and get comfortable with the promises you make to your customers.

"WHAT I LACK IN TALENT, I COMPENSATE WITH MY WILLINGNESS TO GRIND IT OUT. THAT'S THE SECRET OF MY LIFE."
—*Guy Kawasaki*

Guy Kawasaki's book, *Enchantment: The Art of Changing Hearts, Minds, and Actions,* is the inspiration for this drum's name. Others might call it excitement or marketing, but I think these terms miss the point. To me, the word "enchantment" captures the essence of your market-centric activities within the DRUMBEAT Framework:

What messaging makes your company impossible to resist?
What makes people call you first?
What keeps them from trying someone or something else?
What solves their problem so easily that they wouldn't dream of wasting any of their precious time finding your replacement on THEIR weekly BEAT Sheet?

ARE YOU FOCUSED ENOUGH ON MARKETING?
Chief Outsiders, the fractional CMO group, conducted a study of CEOs of small- and medium-size businesses. The study found that many tended to underperform when compared with their competitors. Why? Because they spent most of their time in operations and not enough in marketing. They were neglecting the Enchantment Drum for the Money Drum.

One of the first things I ask my CEO clients is to tell me the percentage of time they spend on operations-centric activities versus market-centric. Nearly all of them respond with something like 80/20. Then I usually smile, hold out my hand and flip it over, meaning 20/80 is the goal.

"BECAUSE THE PURPOSE OF BUSINESS IS TO CREATE
A CUSTOMER, THE BUSINESS ENTERPRISE HAS TWO—
AND ONLY TWO—BASIC FUNCTIONS: MARKETING AND
INNOVATION. MARKETING AND INNOVATION PRODUCE

RESULTS; ALL THE REST ARE COSTS. MARKETING IS THE DISTINGUISHING, UNIQUE FUNCTION OF THE BUSINESS."

—*Peter Drucker*

Before we get any more enchanting Beats in, let's define some terms. Capital "M" marketing is your capital "S" Strategy for creating customers. All Marketing exists to identify qualified leads. It's the job of Sales to close the deal. There is some overlap between day-to-day small "m" marketing and small "s" sales, which we'll discuss later. For now, let's get back to the enchantment spell.

A lot of Red Hat Thinking happens in the Enchantment Drum. Gut feelings, emotions, and intuition are all necessary to understand what's going on at the point of sale. Empathy is required to dance in your customers' shoes, listen like your audience, and think like your client.

In effect, you are in a relationship with your clients, so enchanting them doesn't stop at the point of sale. If you under-promise and over-deliver to them, they will likely tell their friends—and become fiercely loyal to your brand. Take your inspiration from the Rascal Flatts song "Why Wait?"

RASCULS

In his classic book *Influence: The Psychology of Persuasion*, Robert Cialdini describes six primary biases that are hard-wired into humans. I made up the mnemonic acronym RASCLS to remember them:

Reciprocity—If someone does us a favor, we feel obliged to return it.

Authority—If an expert or knowledgeable speaker recommends the product or service, then we tend to believe that the product has value.

Social Proof—If there are many other users, then we tend to think that the product must be great.

Consistency—We've always used this brand, we might not be sure why, but we always will.

Likability—Yes, it really is important to smile!

Scarcity—If we're worried supply will run out, we're more inclined to buy. (By the way, it is unethical to lie about Scarcity. Really, how can you run out of anything digital?)

In his new book *Pre-suasion: Channeling Attention for Change*, Cialdini added a seventh bias. Luckily for me, it still fits in with the other RASCLS: It's Us, as in tribe; the opposite of you versus me. With Us, the acronym becomes RASCULS. (Apparently these rascals still can't spell!)

When the customer identifies with your story, they enter Cialdini's "Us" bias. They've been enchanted. Take a look at your marketing messaging and see how many of these RASCULS are helping you enchant your customers.

In *The Fortune Cookie Principle: The 20 Keys to a Great Brand Story and Why Your Business Needs One*, Bernadette Jiwa likens your brand story to the fortune inside your product or service cookie. You may have to see how your cookie crumbles before re-telling your brand story.

In one of Jiwa's recent STORY OF TELLING blogs, she asks several Better Sounding Questions. Here are a few that really jumped out at me.

"Why don't the right people already know about your products or services?"

"Who are your ideal customers and where are they spending their time online and offline?"

"What's your First Ten strategy?"

FIRST, TEN

"THIS, IN TWO WORDS, IS THE SECRET OF THE NEW MARKETING. FIND TEN PEOPLE. TEN PEOPLE WHO TRUST YOU/RESPECT YOU/NEED YOU/LISTEN TO YOU . . . THOSE TEN PEOPLE NEED WHAT YOU HAVE TO SELL, OR WANT IT. AND IF THEY LOVE IT, YOU WIN. IF THEY LOVE IT, THEY'LL EACH FIND YOU TEN MORE PEOPLE (OR A HUNDRED OR A THOUSAND OR, PERHAPS, JUST THREE). REPEAT. IF THEY DON'T LOVE IT, YOU NEED A NEW PRODUCT. START OVER."

—Seth Godin

Before going to market with a new product or service, you must first check for signs of life. If cats don't eat the cat food, make sure you're offering the right food to the right cats. Doing so—and finding that one little needed tweak—has made a historic difference for several famous brands.

For example, Betty Crocker cake mix was a flop until someone realized that women wanted to stir in their love by breaking an egg into it. WD40 failed at its aerospace application—but was fantastic at lubricating squeaky door hinges. Febreeze was actually received as an insult to homeowners that their homes smelled bad, until it was re-marketed as the fancy bow on top of a hard morning's cleaning.

Tip: If your company doesn't have a brand story, then you're a commodity. You okay with that?

THE EXECUTION OF MARKETING

Let's say you have a brand story, you fully understand the problems your customers face, and you're keeping your promise to them. You're ready to enchant them, but there are hundreds—if not thousands—of ways to market your business.

What three items should you put in your Enchantment Drum to work on next week? To find out, ask Better Sounding Questions, such as:

1. "What strategy would get us the most new clients the fastest, with the best profit margins?"

2. "Which are the easiest to do quickly (perhaps even just a series of Finales)?"

3. "If there is a difficult project that could reap huge rewards, could we set up a weekly DRUMBEAT that would get it done in a reasonable amount of time?"

While much of what we've discussed can be handled by you and your Band of Characters, you may want to consider hiring a marketing professional. Marketing has, after all, gotten complicated in the digital age. Ask yourself how much more successful your marketing initiative would be if you could get professional help answering any of these questions.

If you think you could benefit from marketing expertise, consider finding someone who can show you solid success stories, and has the confidence that they can do the same for you.

HUNTERS, FARMERS, AND DRUMMERS

There are two classic types of sales people. Hunters try to enchant new clients, and Farmers try to enchant existing clients to buy more goods and services.

Typically, Hunting is more expensive than Farming, due to the cost of travel, material, and limited success rate. Farming costs less because a tie with the client already exists; phone calls and emails can be adequately effective.

But keep in mind that real market share growth comes from hunting, not farming. So while you're comfortably reaping your farming rewards, your competitors are probably out there successfully hunting down new clients.

What do Drummers do? Drummers drum up business! In fact, Drummers usually have talent in hunting, farming, and marketing combined. Drummers start by pulling in as much easy business as they can, by making local sales calls, finding distributors, and using exponential internet platforms like LinkedIn and Facebook.

Remember Bernadette Jiwa's Better Sounding Question, "Where do your ideal customers hang out online and off?" Start with the most logical answer, and figure out ways to get your message into those communities. Try not to work more than a few strategies at once. If one strategy turns into a dead end, move on to a new one, or spend more time on a bright spot that's working. Be a BIG fan of small tests.

HOW TO BEAT YOUR ENCHANTMENT DRUM

If your company is not appearing near the top of the first page of Google search results for your brand or product's main keywords, spend some money with an SEO professional and make it happen. I've seen shockingly good results from this strategy.

Keep in mind, however, that Googling your business name and getting first listing doesn't count as much of a Beat. Instead, focus on keywords your customers use when seeking out your type of product. If you're a plumber in Plattsburgh, then "Plumber Plattsburgh" is a really strong Beat.

After drumming up some easy Beats, try getting publicity with trade magazines or local newspapers. Again, this is where a little money spent with professionals will likely pay off many times over. Consider volunteering to be on a panel, or hold a workshop at a trade show. These actions can result in a higher yield than being an exhibitor. Writing a high quality blog on your website and posting it on social media can reap amazing results. And if you aren't a good writer, find one. There are lots of talented people who you can hire locally, or through an online freelancer platform.

Now, in the case of B2B, identify the ten companies you really would like as customers. Send these ten companies hand written notes, a book, or amusing items (always with impeccable taste) that are related to their business. Use overnight delivery for these items. Be relentless. At some point, one or two will talk with you. Always be likable. I've seen best customers created this way.

A great Drummer should also keep track of the answers to customer questions and objections. This is the continuation of your brand story. It may be that the brand story in your head is not the story your client-facing team members are telling your customers. That's on you too, so fix it. Which story is better?

As in Rod Stewart's song "Every Picture Tells a Story," every interaction a customer has with your company tells your story, too. Is it the one you want told? Can you think of a picture that tells the story your prospective customers want to see? This is a great exercise. When you find one, use it everywhere you can.

Tip: Farmers often don't have the personality to also hunt for new customers. So, it's best practice to hire Hunters or Drummers with some hunting skills for new client acquisition.

DIGITAL CONTENT VS. DIGITAL DISTRIBUTION

Here's a Better Sounding Question. Do you have a digital content problem or a digital distribution problem? It's best not to try to solve both problems at the same time, or even with the same people. You'll want to hold someone accountable for white papers, columns, blogs—and someone else for audience interactions and metrics.

If one Beat is poor and five Beats is outstanding, what grade do you give yourself for your digital marketing? If you're trying to be a maestro, anything under four Beats isn't acceptable. Here again, it pays to hire a digital marketing expert who can handle one problem, or both.

THAT RABBIT HOLE

Once a lead has been qualified—but before it has closed—therein lies the rabbit hole of marketing versus sales.

Be wary of letting Hunters and Farmers do too much marketing. Many sales people will blame bad marketing as an excuse for not making quota, whether it's true or not. By all means, however, give your sales people the opportunity to be involved in marketing campaigns, and to modify your email templates into their own voice. But much of your sales funnel should be automated within a sophisticated marketing process that centers on the personas in your gig drum.

THE PURPLE COW WHO JUMPED OVER THE MOON

If no one sees your marketing, it doesn't matter how good it is. In *Purple Cow: Transform Your Business By Being Remarkable*, Seth Godin makes this point:

> "IN A CROWDED MARKETPLACE, FITTING IN IS FAILING.
> IN A BUSY MARKETPLACE, NOT STANDING OUT
> IS THE SAME AS BEING INVISIBLE."
> —*Seth Godin*

Whatever your marketing message, be sure it stands out in some tasteful way. I can't tell you how many business people I meet who play it too safe; their messages are actually "hiding in plain sight." But business isn't a witness protection program. If you're an introvert, hang out with an extrovert. Find a way to get comfortable with getting noticed. It could turn out to be your moonshot marketing move.

THE OPPOSITE OF ENCHANTMENT

In the hotel industry, a "Queen complex" is when the hotel owner and staff begin to think that their guests should feel honored that they're allowed to stay here. This may work if you truly are The Queen. Otherwise, it's a really bad attitude. Disenchantment from narcissists smells pretty nasty pretty quick.

Many "Queen complex" operators can't understand why, if their product is so great, people aren't buying it. The answer is that they need to stop expecting to be treated as the Queen, and instead to treat each guest like a Queen or King.

Here are two other examples of the Queen Complex that just happened to me. I was asking a store clerk a question when her manager interrupted and had an extended conversation on another topic—while I waited. This happened again, in a different store when a team member offered to move a piece of equipment that was in my way. A manager started to help, but then proceeded to block me in for a few minutes while they got their schedules straight. I just smiled, listened, and observed the Queen complex in action. If you want to be supremely productive, take care of the customers or clients or guests first, and have your Jam sessions after they've moved along.

Instead of waving to the masses the way The Queen does, hold out your hand in welcome. Spend more time enchanting—and less time executing tasks which can be delegated to others. If you don't think others can deliver the experience required, stay tuned: The next and last Do-ing Drum is Teamwork.
\

CHAPTER REVIEW

The market-centric activities in the Enchantment Drum are frequently underplayed by business owners. But the only way to grow your business is to increase sales. Having an irresistible brand story and living up to that promise sets you up for a really strong Beat. Focusing on a few of the most important high potential channels will get better results than doing a lot of stuff just because everyone else is. A really strong Beat on the Enchantment Drum will get you heard by potential customers. Without that, it's really hard to kick your business up to the next level.

\|

THREE BEATS TO REMEMBER

\   Do you have a compelling brand story to enchant your customers?

| Focus on only a few high yield activities, done correctly, for best results.

/   It doesn't really matter if the growth comes from marketing or sales.

\|/

PRACTICE

Individuals

Make a list entitled "What inspires the customer to purchase?" Fill it in.

Teams/Band of Characters

Group Discussion: Share your "What inspires the customer to purchase?" lists. Narrow these ideas down to the best three inspirations. Start with those.

Large companies

Compile ways to respond to these best inspirations lists from each department.

\|//

Enchantment Drum Notes

Score your top four ideas for Marketing.
Make one of them a picture, a visual story, to enchant new users.

1	2	3	4

Enchantment Drum Notes

Score your top four ideas for Sales.

1	2	3	4

CHAPTER 13

// Teamwork Drum

THE REMAINING DO-ING SKILL DRUM, the Teamwork Drum, is how you fit in with your team, how you relate, when to follow, and when to lead. This Drum also encompasses building character into yourself and your Band of Characters, finding your mojo, and determining how your team fits into the company you're keeping. It's your . . . House of Conversation.

Let's take it from the top. When it comes down to it, what do you really have to offer your team? Your thinking, your words, and your actions. In the words of former long-time Vistage chair Susan Scott:

"THE CONVERSATION IS THE RELATIONSHIP."

—*Susan Scott, Fierce Conversations: Achieving Success at Work & in Life,*
One Conversation at a Time

Hang on. Read that again: "The conversation IS the relationship."

Think about this for a minute: If you don't put time and effort into your conversations, then you are diminishing your relationships. In fact, you might be something of a narcissist. Or maybe you're just not very interesting. Ouch! On the other hand, if people aren't listening to you, or they're splitting their attention with their mobile phones, they too might be narcissists.

Conversations matter. A lot. So before you start talking, spend some time finding the right words. Think of every conversation as a negotiation with essentially four possible outcomes:

1. Both the other person and you fail (a lose-lose)

2. You win and the other person loses (win-lose)

3. You lose and the other person wins (lose-win)

4. You both benefit (win-win).

Were there any successful team members on the TITANIC? Are there any unsuccessful team members on the Super Bowl Championship Team?

Winning matters. Here's what it looks like in drum notation:

1234 1234 1234 1234 1234 1234
W I N W I N
LRLR_R_RLR__LRLR_R_RLR__

It's worth a little planning to find a path to win/win before starting any conversation with your team.

HOUSE OF HIRING

Hiring: The Science vs. The Art

For years I was ambivalent about hiring assessments. I've seen these scientific tools work—and not work—for various companies. Following Productivity Riff #18: Be a BIG fan of small tests, I have now come to the conclusion that scientific hiring assessments work.

These scales come in roughly three types: personality assessments, cognition assessments, and skill assessments. I'll leave the skill testing to you. For personality, it appears that testing candidates blind is probably best practice. As in the TV show "The Voice," candidates should move to the next round only when they are deserving—not just because they're charismatic or extroverted.

At the very least, try to match the personality type to the position. As you gain experience with these tools, you'll know which personality types have a better chance of success. Personality surveys are relatively cheap and sometimes free. They may create a win-win for you when it comes to moving people into specific positions.

Cognition tests involving letters, numbers, and abstract reasoning are usually more expensive and can be reserved for later rounds in your hiring process. They are probably best used after completing structured interviewing. To choose an effective cognition assessment, look for platforms that have a robust backend that can help manage your team's strengths, abilities, and personality-blending strategies.

Now, here's the argument for the Art of Hiring: the use of intuition, innate personality understanding, or anything else that involves interpretation of someone's "vibe." You may have someone on your team—maybe yourself—who is a fantastic judge of character without ever having used an assessment tool. If you're not experiencing team problems operating this way, then by all means keep doing what's working and move on to another drum.

Whatever methods you use, the only way to know what works best for your team is to keep records of turnover and performance for those hired by both the Art and Science methods. If you don't measure the results, you'll never know which is best. Why does that matter? Because your competitors are probably already leveraging assessments to build better teams.

Keep in mind that you may spend less time and money testing hiring assessments than you lose in having management debate their use. You may be wrong, or you may be right. There's only one way to find out, so remember Productivity Riff #2: In the time it took to worry about it, it could've been done!

ARE YOUR MANAGERS ACTUALLY LEADERS?

In the DRUMBEAT, we distinguish between the person in authority and the person exhibiting leadership. These concepts comprise a field called adaptive leadership and are addressed specifically in *Leadership Without Easy Answers* by Ronald Heifetz.

Here's an example. When I was CEO of the hotel company, the corporate offices were on the second floor of one of the properties. One snowy New Jersey morning, I got to work early and looked out the window at the departing guests.

Miguel the Bellman (not his real name) was shoveling paths to the guests' driver side car doors, and using a push broom to clear the snow off the hoods and windshields. This task was not in the employee manual. We were sold out last night, and there were well over a hundred cars in the lot.

I walked downstairs and found the General Manager in his office reading the daily report. He was doing nothing wrong; he was pounding the Prediction Drum. But he was not exhibiting leadership. Miguel was. Miguel, not the GM, was solving our guests' problems. Miguel was also making well-deserved tips from grateful travelers.

When you're cruising with your Trio, your Band of Characters, your team, in the company you keep, and in your House of Thinking, take a minute to see who is exhibiting leadership—and who is merely using their power. Leadership beats management in the long run.

HOUSE OF THINKING

In essence, the driving question for this Drum is "How do we win together?" or, phrased by virtuoso coach Marshall Goldsmith, "How can I help our team succeed?" When everyone keeps this question foremost in their minds, everyone is suddenly dancing to the same Beat! In terms of teamwork, you could actually call it your Drum Circle. (Before book's end we'll discuss whether a literal drum circle is right for your team.)

> "MOJO IS THAT POSITIVE SPIRIT TOWARD WHAT WE ARE DOING NOW, THAT STARTS FROM THE INSIDE AND RADIATES TO THE OUTSIDE."
> — *Marshall Goldsmith*

HOUSE OF THE RISING CONFLICT

Thinking and acting like a team will go a long way. But beware that if you go too far, you may fall off the "groupthink" cliff. This is where everyone green-lights a terrible decision in a kumbaya moment. This is also sometimes referred to as a false equivalence. Cabbage is tasty. Chocolate is delicious. But would your customers ever order chocolate-covered cabbage? When no one wants to be the naysayer, bad decisions can be made.

On the other hand, debating issues has its limitations too. The alpha extroverts, those in authority, almost always win. Why shouldn't they? For one, they might be flat out wrong. Next, if people aren't empowered to make their own decisions, they'll never learn from their mistakes. It's much more fun to gossip about the boss's mistakes than to try to avoid your own. I know you want to run a fun house, but go ahead and try a little empowerment and a little creative conflict instead.

Ultimately, it isn't always possible to find a win-win, and it isn't a great idea to have a room full of yes-people. So let's spend some time on the importance of creative conflict.

CREATIVE CONFLICT BETWEEN INDIVIDUALS

How should you deal with conflict? The short answer: Ask questions. A lot of questions. Here are some creative ways to not only resolve disagreements, but leverage them to your company's advantage.

SIX THINKING HATS—PLUS THREE

Over the years, I've discovered three additional Thinking Hats to add to de Bono's original six, which we discussed earlier. The gap between the Yellow Thinking Hat (the best case scenario) and the Black Thinking Hat (the worst-case) is sometimes too large.

The Purple Thinking Hat, much like the Prediction Drum, is what's probably going to happen. It's the default, or the most likely scenario. In the sequence, it's Yellow, Black, and Purple (for probable).

Go back to the conflicting White Thinking Hat facts. Because things are so complicated today, the Team should spend some time with their Grey Thinking Hats on. I can't tell you how many times I've seen a quick great decision made just by wiping the gray grime off murky facts. Conflicting items should get placed in the Grey Thinking Hat to be resolved before putting on your Blue Thinking Hats for the next steps.

Often during a process, someone on the team will realize that we might be on the wrong question. Maybe there's a Better Sounding Question. The Orange Thinking Hat question is, "Aren't we processing the wrong question?" or "Orange we trying to solve the wrong puzzle?" Anyone can put on the Orange Thinking Hat to raise this question. Wear this Orange cap carefully—but wear it proudly. Now you're thinking!

We are all living in a cacophony of messages, ads, memes, propaganda, and product choices. Maybe that's what Bob Dylan was talking about in his song "Leopard-Skin Pill-Box Hat"!

THE SOUND OF THINKING

Albert Einstein once said that you can't solve a problem using the same mindset that created it. Here's where things get a little dicey. We need to do a little thinking about thinking . . . before we start thinking. Consider some of these questions:

How has another industry solved this problem?

How have our competitors solved the problem?

Have we solved a similar but different problem successfully before?

When do we really need a decision?

Who needs to be involved?

Do we need to diverge and gather more info first? (More on this in a moment.)

Wasting bandwidth on the wrong topics, low quality thinking, or half-baked efforts is the opposite of being productive.

FIVE WAYS TO CURE TEAM DYSFUNCTION

Creative conflict resolution is extremely important to your DRUMBEAT. So important, in fact, that here's another take. In *The Five Dysfunctions of a Team: A Leadership Fable,* author Patrick Lencioni explains the commonly untapped advantage of organizational health. He refers to often-overlooked workplace essentials such as minimal politics and confusion, plus high morale and productivity—which can together result in lower turnover. This leads to the five behaviors to cure team dysfunctions:

- Building trust
- Mastering conflict
- Achieving commitment
- Embracing accountability
- Focusing on results.

Which behaviors does your Band of Characters need to work on?

Here's my favorite concept of Lencioni's: Over-communicating. Given adult learning behavior, a new concept needs to be heard more than five times to be understood by the listener. We are bombarded with messages all day, everyday. How are we supposed to hear the DRUMBEAT? How is your Band of Characters going to stay in your rhythm? Only by you not letting them forget what you really care about.

CONVERGENCE VS. DIVERGENCE

There are two phases in a meeting—divergence and convergence. During divergence, you're trying to fairly assess and analyze the situation. During convergence you are seeking answers. If you start to converge too early, the neuroscience is clear: The anchoring or priming on a solution shuts down our executive functions—and we actually stop thinking.

Years ago, I wrote a column for *Hotel Management Magazine* saying, "Don't just employ your team's hours. Employ their minds!" Diverge before converging.

MEETING FLOWS

If you are in a position of authority, here are some good habits: In the divergent part of a meeting in which everyone is gathering facts and talking about options, the goal is for everyone to participate.

Be careful not to wrap a solution in a too-clever question. But in the convergence portion of the meeting, when you all are trying to find a solution and where you are the person of authority, try as hard as you can to speak last.

Here's why, using the three possible outcomes.

First, if your team arrives at a great solution, you won't have risked any social capital by participating, and you're the superstar for letting the team shine. If you have a tendency to micromanage, this is a great antidote.

Second, if the team arrives at a barely-okay solution, then they'll have a chance to learn from their mistakes, and you get to see who is and isn't thinking. You can also keep an eye out for the first sign that it was a mediocre decision—and do a check-in with the group to ask them how it's going. Then you'll begin to see who is really paying attention to the win.

Last, if the team is struggling, waiting until the end gives you more time to consider all the different viewpoints and to mentally cycle through the Nine Thinking Hats. You may very well come up with the Crash-Through that solves the problem. That's why you're the maestro, or at least the boss!

These three outcomes are a Win Storm. The only downside is a little time spent to develop your team into a well-oiled thinking machine.

Just as in Simon and Garfunkel's song "The Sound of Silence," treasure the silence between speakers when meeting with your team. Learn to let silence do the heavy lifting. These lyrics, besides putting an ironic exclamation point on your silence, have actual neuroscience backing them. The whispers you hear are messages from your Chief Thinking Officer (your subconscious, which never sleeps). Where do you think all your good ideas come from, anyway?

Peter Drucker says culture eats strategy for breakfast. Vistage speaker Gustavo Grodnitzky wrote a wonderful book called *Culture Trumps Everything: The Unexpected Truth about*

the Ways Environment Changes Biology, Psychology, and Behavior.
The DRUMBEAT says . . .

Spouse Eats Strategy for Supper

I'm suggesting this litmus test for your culture: When one of your team members sits down to dinner with family and explains what happened at work today, your culture is what the spouse says or thinks next. Your team member is now smack dab in the tension between your strategy and their company culture.

In Chapter 11, the Money Drum, we discussed Tribal Leadership and its five types of culture. The goal is for these dinner conversations not to devolve into "Life Sucks" or "My Life Sucks."

Bob Chapman, CEO of Barry-Wehmiller, suggests this spouse litmus test in a ten-minute video on the crisis in leadership. You might screen it first, and then share it with your key reports. Show your Band of Characters some love.

In other words, what ill-advised policy was put into effect today? What subtle messages are you sending that communicate that you don't trust your team? When making a decision, have you neglected to include someone who should have had input? What decisions are you making with the Red Thinking Hat, or worse, the leopard-skin pill-box hat?

STRUCTURING TEAMS

In Chapter 7, we discussed the Four Stages of Competency: Student, Amateur, Maestro and Virtuoso. Here is a teamwork story that highlights the importance of having a student on every work team.

An older property had a bad odor coming from the basement. The crawl spaces were quite tight and difficult to navigate. A plumbing company was brought in. They couldn't find the source of the problem, but they still sent a bill for their time.

Next, an engineering firm was brought in. $3000 later they decided the smell must be emanating from the dirt.

Now the plumbing firm was brought back again and instructed to do whatever it took with as many people as it took—and this was a make-good no charge visit. Ten plumbers arrived, all suited up in environmental jumpers. Ten plumbers searched under the house for an hour.

Finally, a muffled, "I found it!" was heard from deep in the maze. An apprentice wiggled out from under the building, saying he'd discovered a chamber around a corner. That chamber featured an open grease pit. It was the apprentice's first day.

None of the other geniuses, engineers, masters, or journeymen had thought it important enough to look around that corner.

Your lesson? Have a newbie on every team, to ask not-so-dumb questions like, "What's around this corner?"

The best teams have a mix of experience, subject matter expertise, and a beginner's open, inquisitive mind. On any given day, on any given problem, any one or a combination will get you to a better solution. When teams truly mesh, they have a fantastic Beat!

Sounding a clear Beat on the Teamwork Drum will assure that you don't end up with an orchestra of soloists with no sheet music.

END OF THE LINE

Whole books have been and will continue to be written on firing employees. I contend that if you have smart, caring people who embrace the company's values, value propositions, and processes, you'll have fantastic outcomes. At minimum, regular conversations are necessary to find a solution. This could be an offer to help, switch positions, or find a new company. Consider having three-way conversations as opposed to one-to-ones with the boss. I'm a BIG fan of Trios. When two people are talking, at least one is REALLY listening, and you can compare notes later.

\

CHAPTER REVIEW

The only reason to have a team is to win. Your role as Master Drummer is to instill in every team member an attitude of "How can I help my team win?" The way to win in business is through the successful resolution of creative conflict. Using tools like the Six Thinking Hats, combined with good meeting habits, can help you accomplish this. A culture shift toward thinking and away from reacting will assure your Teamwork Drum is in a synchronized Beat with your Strategy Drum.

\|

THREE BEATS TO REMEMBER

\ How can I help my team win?

| Find healthy ways to resolve team conflict.

/ Be intentional when setting up teams to solve problems.

\|/

PRACTICE

Individuals

Ask your Trio "How can I help my team win?" (based on Marshall Goldsmith's work).

Team/Band of Characters

Ask everyone, individually, "How can I help our team win?" Then shut up and listen. You may hear some ideas that will be humbling. Sleep on it. Then decide how to take action.

Large companies

Gather up all of your department heads. Repeat the exercise, "How can I help our team win?"

\|//

Teamwork Drum Notes

Score your top four ideas to improve hiring.

1	2	3	4

Teamwork Drum Notes

Score your top four Team Building ideas.

1	2	3	4

PART FIVE

YOUR METAL

CHAPTER 14

// *The Steel Drum*

THE STEEL DRUM IS BOTH A DRUM AND A STRONG METAL. Unlike the other seven Skill Drums that are either Be-ing or Do-ing, the Steel Drum is both. The Steel Drum holds your 1 to 3 primary weekly projects that steal time away from all the other drums—in a good way. You will be almost totally immersed in your Steel Drum project.

> "THE GOOD LORD MADE US ALL OUT OF IRON, THEN HE TURNS UP THE HEAT TO FORGE SOME OF US INTO STEEL."
> —*Marie Osmond*

These are the projects that, if played correctly, will move both your audience and your career. And you'll need a steel backbone to keep this backbeat up! But don't worry there will be more on your backbeat, soon.

STEEL DRUMS FOR EVERYONE

It's a great idea to not only pick YOUR Steel Drum projects wisely, but to know what your team members have in THEIR Steel Drums for the week. Beware, however, of Steel Drum projects that are red herrings, white whales, or rabbit holes. This steals time from the other Skill Drums in a bad way.

There is controversy over how many primary projects someone should tackle in a week. Some pundits say one. Others say two, and still others, three. I think it's a matter of style, and we'll go into greater detail on styles in Chapter 18. More than three projects in one week might work for you, but usually that gets pretty confusing pretty quickly.

MY STYLE

Personally, I like two, sometimes maybe briefly three. The first two major projects give me an opportunity to switch to the other when I get stuck. The third allows me to skip a day or two on a project and come back at it fresh. Two 90-minute deep drumming Sessions in a day gives you a day off for the second or third Steel Drum project. It gives your Chief Thinking Officer a chance to find the Beat for you. Thank you, CthinkO!

I also try to keep my 60-minute Jam Sessions, 30-minute Finales!, and 4 minute Warm-ups on the same general topics as the one or two Steel Drum items for the day.

Frequently I can have a very productive 90-minute Solo Session in the late afternoon. If I'm fatigued, sometimes it can be unusually creative as my conscious filters are off and the CthinkO is closer to the surface. If the muse is missing,

I switch to numbers instead of letters. We'll discuss more of these productivity tips in Chapter 18.

STEEL DRUM ACCOUNTABILITY

Here's a best practice from Vistage speaker Mike "Accountability" Scott: Check with every key report, every week on the three most important strategic items on your plate.

> "DON'T CHEAT YOUR PEOPLE OUT OF THE OPPORTUNITY
> TO WIN BECAUSE OF YOUR DISCOMFORT
> HOLDING PEOPLE ACCOUNTABLE."
> —*Michael Canic*

In other words, know where all the Steel Drum projects are in the scheme of things. It can take as little as a 15-minute standing Jam session with your Band of Characters. Knowing you have to identify and report on your priorities to the boss and the team will get everyone to focus on their Steel Drum projects.

If someone needs to revisit an item for accountability, then there's a Two-Way discussion. Super coach Steve Chandler talks about having constructive agreements versus having toxic expectations. In a genuine discussion, both parties need to agree on what they will do to make sure the desired outcome happens.

Personally, I think the biggest problem with accountability is that the boss heaps so much onto their direct reports that no one can hear the darn Beat. When these Beats don't align, that's a great item for the top of the Jam Session.

Take a look at the drum breaks below. Which best visually represents the DRUMBEAT you're giving your team?
Left (\) = Your Team. Right (/) = You

`/////\ // \ \ // \ \ // \ // \\//\\// \ // \ \ // \ \ // \ //`
`///\/\/\\\\\\ //\        /        \\/\\\//\\///////////////`

Which one looks like agreements and which like expectations? Which looks like work and which like play? Which like a team and which like micromanaging? The top has rhythm the bottom is just noise. Noise is tiring.

How about this DRUMBEAT?

`//`

Not enough reinforcement. It sounds like, "I told you once four months ago I needed you to do blank. What's wrong with you?" If it was really that important it bears repeating. That's on you. You can almost never repeat the core values, mission, and DRUMBEAT to your team too much.

Of the 7 Skill Drums, we need to make sure the Strategy Drum's question "How will we win?" is in everyone's Steel Drum, and make sure they're keeping that Beat. If they aren't, that's on you for not checking each week. This is a liberating exercise. It forces the boss to make sure everyone's in rhythm right down the line.

`\`

CHAPTER REVIEW

Of all the Better Sounding Questions you're working on in your 7 Skill Drums, at least the most important from your Strategy Drum should be promoted to your Steel Drum project of the week. This project will get first dibs on the 90-minute Solo Sessions each day to make sure you make progress. Depending on your style you might have one or two other primary projects to focus on as well. It's imperative for you to know what your team's Steel Drum projects are, and to keep them accountable. We'll talk more about how in the next chapter.

\|

THREE BEATS TO REMEMBER

\ The Steel Drum project is the most important to assure the team wins.

| Steel Drum projects get first dibs on 90-minute Solo Sessions.

/ The team needs to keep track of their Steel Drum progress together.

\|/

PRACTICE

Individuals

Pick your Steel Drum project for next week and discuss it with the boss.

Teams (Your Band of Characters)

Start a habit of meeting early and later in the week to discuss the status of everyone's Steel Drum projects.

Large Companies

Do a monthly assessment of everyone's Steel Drum projects and make sure they are in alignment with the overall strategy for winning.

\ | //

STEEL DRUM NOTES

In a normal week you get ten 90-minute Solo Sessions. How might you decide which projects to put in your Steel Drum and how many Solo sessions to schedule?

STEEL DRUM NOTES

Check with the boss and your Band of Characters and see what their Steel Drum projects are, and if you need to support them with Solo sessions of your own.

CHAPTER 15

// Four Cymbals to Crash-Through

WE NOW KNOW FROM NEUROSCIENCE that habits are far more important in behavior than previously thought. We also know that mental models are needed to navigate around our biases in order to outsmart ever-increasing daily complexities.

We only get about three hours a day for truly deep, quality thinking. This is where our drumsticks make surprising sounds. This is where they crash into the metal cymbals—the mental symbols of winning moves. They also test the mettle of our character, along with our personal focus and drive. This is as much art as it is science.

There are critical points in any drumroll when the deep sounds of the drums need to be accented with the clarity and surprise of the metal cymbals. The same is true in our framework. You need to ride the cymbals until you can Crash-Through to the next step . . . and the next. These are the three-move strategies that will bump your game up to the next level.

In *SWITCH: How to Change Things When Change is Hard*, authors Chip and Dan Heath refer to a concept called "Script the Critical Moves." I call it the next three Crash-Throughs. Chess Grandmasters think strategically about four moves out by choosing a general strategy for an advantage, the best first move based on mental models, and then a path to a decisive advantage. Billiard players script out their critical moves as well: They plan for which side of the fourth ball they want to be on in order to have the next four ball run.

We can do this too. The Four Cymbals, from left to right on the BEAT Sheet, are:

The First Crash-Through
Ride the Cymbal-ic How
What's the TaDa!?
Symbolic Reward

But you plan for them in this order:

What's the TaDa!?
The First Crash-Through
Ride the Cymbal-ic How
Symbolic Reward

CRASH-THROUGH EXAMPLE—WRITING A BOOK

Once I finished the outline for this book, I set a Steel Drum project for each of the next 20 weeks: "How to Script the

Chapter?" Each week my What's the TaDa!? third cymbal was "a chapter a week." The First Crash-Through was to get up every morning between 4am and 5am to write.

My second Crash-Through, the Ride the Cymbal-ic How?, was any combination of these: Follow the outline, follow the muse, improv, read a book for research, scan studies, adapt a blog piece, look for connections, and listen to podcasts for inspiration. Every week was different, but patterns emerged to keep breaking on through to the other side.

My Symbolic Reward for completing a chapter was a workout or a nice lunch. I repeated a similar process for the first edit.

That was my Steel Drum Beat for The DRUMBEAT !!

CRASH-THROUGH EXAMPLE — STARTUP BUSINESS

Here's a mentoring session I once did for a startup business:

The first Crash-Through in your strategy has to do with "Proof of Life" for your project. It appears that you need a critical mass of distributors happily using your website and app so there's enough robust activity to stick with it.

Your Plan A is free for a year. But that is not risk-free. There are lots of free word processor and spreadsheet programs, yet Microsoft Office still prevails and has done so for decades. So that's not a sure-fire plan. What is your Plan B and your Plan C?

Venture Capital (VC) investors will be much more likely to invest once you are successfully past your first Crash-Through "Proof of Life." But you may already have all the capital you need to get to that Crash Point, anyway. You will give up less equity and control this way as well. So a Better Sounding Question is, "How fast can you get to a critical mass of happy dealer users?"

It may take only a few months. How could you do that in six weeks? Could you do it by this Friday? If you were in a race to the Crash-Through, what would your competitor do? Consider doing that.

See how useful a Crash-Through is? When you get to the Crash Point, you'll either hit a wall, or you'll crash-through to the other side.

RECAP

The timeline of a Steel Drum Project may occur over several weeks or months, but each week it's necessary to have a specific weekly goal. We know now that small wins are very important to keep motivation high. As you saw in this example, it even builds habits as sub-routines that kick in almost automatically to get through roadblocks.

THE FIRST CRASH-THROUGH

The first Crash-Through is as important as the last. What's the first step? One big mistake most people make is to think of things in groups, or in otherwise abstract terms. It's highly unlikely you can get 100 things done before lunch. The first Beat in a long drumroll to a critical mass of users is talking with a single person. It's also wise to listen to their Beat carefully.

RIDE THE CYMBAL-IC HOW

The second step is usually pounding on the Enchantment Drum. The Enchantment Drum's simple question is, "What inspires the audience?" Making a presentation to a trade association group of prospective users is a great middle step. Be sure you've thought through the answer to every possible question you can imagine. Write great copy. Know what you're talking about.

WHAT'S THE TADA!?

In Malcolm Gladwell's *The Tipping Point: How Little Things Can Make a Big Difference*, he states for an idea to tip or to just fall into fruition, three factors and one condition must exist. This requires a collector of data, a collector of people, and a collector of answers. Then when the group grows to around 150 people, all the conditions are ripe for the adoption of the idea or product. Let's call that a successful "first concert."

In our business startup example, the conditions to meet are:

- The data needs to fully support the technical competence of the website,
- The critical mass of users would likely need to be around 150 distributors, and
- All the questions of those first users need to be satisfactorily answered.

Now, that's just the Map of the first three Crash-Throughs. Improvisation will happen along the way, but identifying the

Crash Points makes it much easier to think strategically and to have conversations with your team. Since you'll be making course corrections along the way, you may have to revisit the Innovation Drum.

SYMBOLIC REWARDS

The Symbolic Reward you choose must mean something to you. Maybe you're doing this for your kids; then keep one of your kid's toys on your desk. Maybe ice cream is your treat. Or a special dinner out. Or maybe it's just your Rallying Cry.

When you win, call your coach and gloat. Run up stairs then do a Rocky victory dance. Celebrate small wins. Perhaps a really big reward for the whole project would be a vacation, a car, or a nicer health club membership. Your Symbolic Reward should be whatever motivates you!

"THE VOICE" EXAMPLE

Ever hear the famous story about the UPC barcode inventor who threw a plastic flying disc through a scanner—and the price still rang up? In the book *SWITCH*, this is called "See, Feel, Change." In other words, telling people about technical specs is not as effective as showing them an emotional presentation. (I still don't understand why almost every time I get groceries, one item doesn't scan. But that's somebody else's DRUMBEAT to worry about.)

Let's look at one more example of the Metals. The TV show "The Voice" has as its crescendo Crash Point, the TaDa! of finding the winner for the season. The first Crash Point is listening to the contestants without looking at them. The middle Crash Point is totally about "feel." It's like ham on rye . . . an emotional sandwich on logic . . . pathos on a logos roll . . . art on two slices of science.

I'm a big fan of "The Voice." Here is a list of all the emotions and feelings I observed during a typical episode: Overcoming adversity, hope, quest, courage, fun, good-heartedness, friendship, team spirit, generosity, tolerance, support, risk-taking, learning from failure, rooting for the underdog, coaching, mastery, and pride.

That covers the "feel" portion of the program. Why does that matter? Remember that "American Idol" was the market leader when "The Voice" appeared. Arguably, the gentler, kinder overall tone of "The Voice" was a counterpoint to Idol's less tactful tone.

Early on, "The Voice" struggled because their winners were not breakout successes. So they made course adjustments between the first and last Crash-Throughs— and now their artists appear on the pop charts regularly.

BACKBEAT

In rock and roll, the backbeat is a heavy emphasis on the second and fourth Beats. Following that model, these are "Riding the Cymbal-ic How" and the "Symbolic Reward." The good news? The first and third Beats of the week (the First Crash-Through and the TaDa!) are relatively easy. Just pick a "Goal" and get started! Then stay focused on the "Reward" and the trickier "How" will finally appear.

\

CHAPTER REVIEW

Once you know your Steel Drum project, it's best to plan the TaDa! for the week, then the first small step to get started. Then improvise *how* during the 90-minute Solo sessions. The more quality time you can practice, the more new insights and deeper understanding of the project you'll get. Having a Symbolic Reward for completing each weekly TaDa! is a big motivator, so enjoy these wins! As you get used to the new rhythms, you might find that juggling two or three Steel Drum projects to be your best DRUMBEAT. Remember to put feeling into your "how." It will give you an unmistakable backbeat!

\|

THREE BEATS TO REMEMBER

\ Pick your Week's TaDa!, your first step, and block sufficient Solo sessions.

| Once into the How, remember to put some feeling into it.

/ Stay motivated and celebrate weekly wins with Symbolic Rewards.

\|/

PRACTICE

Individuals

Plan out your Crash-Throughs for next week. Review them with the boss.

Teams (Your Band of Characters)

Review everyone's Crash-Throughs from last week, and discuss what worked and what didn't. Tweak for the following week.

Large Companies

Have the executive team plan Crash-Throughs for the month or quarter, as the lengths of projects in senior management frequently have longer lead times.

\|//

Steel Drum Notes

What questions in your 7 Skill Drums could be promoted to the Steel Drum this week?

Steel Drum Notes

Assuming you have 10 Three Hour Sets next week, how will you assign the Steel Drum task(s) to 90-minute Solo sessions, 60-minute Jam sessions, and 30-minute Finales!?

PART SIX

WHAT SHOULD I BE-DO-ING RIGHT NOW?

CHAPTER 16

// Your BEAT Sheets

Everything up to now leads to this point. The BEAT Sheets are how we plan for next week and tomorrow. We'll also talk about strategies to use these sheets throughout this chapter. Now we'll see how your DRUMBEAT fits together on one sheet of paper for the week, and another for the next day. The BEAT Sheet is the sheet music for your performance, but you'll be improvising along the way.

At 23 years old, I was the food and beverage director at a very nice, brand-new, brand-name commercial hotel. There were about a dozen department heads and assistants, and almost all of them went home at 5pm, leaving me in charge. I found ordering my priorities throughout the shift to be dizzying. I was on rounds one night when I asked myself the following question for the very first time, and I've never stopped.

"What should I be-do-ing, right now?"

It was invariably something else. Seven years later, I became CEO of a hotel chain with twelve properties. This just might be the best, Better Sounding Question you can ask your productive self! Try it.

Back to our scale of questions, "What should I be doing, right now?" is at one end. "What should I be doing next week?" is at the other.

DAILY BEAT

Let's start with making tomorrow's plan on your Daily BEAT. As mentioned throughout the book your DRUMBEAT Day is based on two 3-hour Sets. Each Set has a 90-minute uninterrupted Solo Session.

The first few uninterrupted 90-minute Solo Sessions might seem a bit weird. You'll be fighting the urge to get that dopamine rush by checking email, social media, or making a quick call. Make these a reward for finishing the 90 minutes. You'll also need to speak with your Band of Characters and explain what happened to your open door policy. I have clients who close their shade along with their door to signify "not yet," and another client who puts a red circle on the door.

Your 60-minute Jam Sessions are to communicate in-person, phone, text, or email. The suggestion here is that email is great for information exchange. Text is excellent for quick questions and answers. Phone is phenomenal for building and maintaining relationships. In-person meetings need to have a serious structure, although in some cases the structure can be intentionally not structured.

The last session in a Set is a half hour for completing quick tasks we call Finales! Remember in the first chapter we talked about the band that never thinks the stage is big enough? There are lots of tasks that really can be completed in very little time. But if someone doesn't have enough to do—or has a very slow DRUMBEAT—they will take as much time as possible. When I started allowing myself only 30 minutes twice a day to do urgent but unimportant tasks, they got done so fast I couldn't believe it.

Let's put it all together. Let's say you're the type of person who likes Sets in a 90-minute, 60-minute, 30-minute order. This is what I call the Snowball style, because on your daily sheet the circles that represent your drums are stacked like snowballs: large on the bottom, then medium, then small. When Snowball sees that there's only 30 minutes, the trick is to think, "I can knock out A, B, and maybe C, and then reward myself with a short walk and lunch." Now that's a DRUMBEAT! If you like to work visually there is a Snowball template to follow in the Appendix on page 262.

But you might be the type of person who likes to get those little things out of the way first, including quick meetings, so you can really focus on your 90-minute Solo Session. The Daily BEAT for you looks like a Tornado. I sometimes call this style "Whiplash" in honor of a really gripping movie about a young drummer's journey from amateur to maestro. The circles that represent Tornado's drums on the Beat sheet are stacked small on the bottom, medium in the middle, and large on top. If you like to work visually there is a Tornado template to follow in the Appendix on page 263.

There are no right or wrong styles. In fact, you may feel like changing styles on any given day, and after awhile you'll realize which is best for you at any given time. That would be a sign you're turning into a master drummer.

The third major style is, well, no style at all. On any given day either Snowball or Whiplash works. Or maybe even start with meetings followed by either a Solo Session or Finales! I call this style Jazz or Juggler because the Daily BEAT looks like throwing all the balls up in the air and seeing which one you catch first. If you like to work visually there is a Juggler template to follow in the Appendix on page 264.

There are a few different techniques for using your Daily BEAT Sheet. You can divide each circle into two, for the before-and-after lunch Sets. Or you can have a clean sheet for each. I've come to have the items for a few days on the whiteboard or LCD eWriter and pick the ones I feel like doing at the moment. I simply cross out and add as needed.

When I started doing this, the board was packed. But once you get into these habits you'll find a lot of white space as you are so productive you're usually caught up, if not looking for new and more interesting projects.

Now let's take a look at your weekly BEAT Sheet before we finish up with your Daily BEAT.

WEEKLY BEAT SHEET

Try to complete your first weekly BEAT Sheet in a single session. You can use the one-page mind map, or set up a digital BEAT Sheet in your favorite note taking program. You can find either in the Appendix. Take a few minutes to choose.

You don't have to over-think this. You'll be getting a chance to edit it almost every week. The most important thing is to get started. I suggest a 90-minute uninterrupted Solo Session. You might finish early or you may need a second Session.

The following is a full review of the Drumbeat Framework. There is a one-page recap in the Appendix. You may prefer the Quick Start Guide, so you can begin seeing productivity gains almost immediately, and add the other functionality as you need it.

What's your Rallying Cry, your core values? Say whatever drives you, in three to five words. This might be for you or for your company. If your Rallying Cry is for your Band of Characters or your team, developing it should be a group exercise. Remember, if you go fast, you go alone. If it is for you, what keeps you going when nothing else will? What are you really great at? What can you do that gives you your own style?

If the Rallying Cry is for your company, then ask, "What are our core values? What sets us apart from the commodity aspects of our business?" Don't forget to have an emotional pull. This Rallying Cry can be your public face, or it can be just for your team as an internal motivator.

What's your company's main Gig? What's your main Gig? Be specific when you finish the sentences, "_____ hires us/me to _____ so s/he can _____."

Don't use: "Customers hire us to fix their pipes so their house doesn't flood."

Instead: "Anxious homeowners call us to arrive within the hour so we can assure them the job will be done right the first time."

This might even let you charge a premium price for your premium service, which will then allow you to save enough for retirement.

The 3- and 1-Year Bass Goal Drums need a metric, a metronome to keep you on the path to your success. Something like 20% growth in 20 months, making up rhymes or Rallying Cries for goals is more than useful—it's a really strong Beat. Some industries are moving so fast you may want to just do the 1-Year Goal to get started. Thinking further out in these industries might just be fiction.

The 90-Day Rock and Role Drums are really important. These break the year into 4/4 time, a very strong rhythm for your team to follow. These goals may be a little less financial and more managerial in nature. It may be that you or your Band of Characters need to perfect a new process. Perhaps you need to add a new dimension to your customer service. In either case, start with 1–3 goals, and over time no more than 4–7.

The Kettle Drum on the one-pager is symbolic; you'll need to set up a separate digital document or a journal. For this exercise put down three ideas under the Notes bar: 1 need-to, 1 want-to, and 1 might. This will give you enough to understand the process. Try to have them be on different topics, in other words not all in the same Skill Drum; which again are Learning, Innovation, Prediction, Strategy, Money, Enchantment, and Teamwork.

You'll need to put into writing your personal Filtering Questions in your Kettle Drum Document. Think of these questions as the way you master the Kettle Drum. This is how you keep an impossible-to-ignore booming Beat.

For now, let's just go with the first default question, "Is this worth my time?"

Let's assume for this exercise that all three are worth your time. Now take one of these Notes and turn it into a question, and a much Better Sounding Question at that. Don't rush this phase. You'll probably know it when you hear it, because you can't answer it without giving your CthinkO a chance to weigh in.

Now take this Better Sounding Question and place it into the most appropriate Skill Drum. Repeat this process with the other two Notes. If you have time, you might want to try to find a Better Sounding Question for each of the 7 Skill Drums.

Let's review: The process is to capture and keep all your Notes in the bottom of the Kettle. Then some will pass through your own Filtering Questions, to be formed into Better Sounding Questions for your Skill Drums. To be well balanced and have a stellar Beat, you'll want at least one item in every drum. Hint: Think about this for a moment, don't all A+ Players you know whale on all seven skill drums?

Now you're moving onto your Steel Drum Project. This is what you will absolutely positively achieve in the coming week, and how you're going to approach it. This is also where you begin to sync your daily and weekly BEAT Sheets.

Pick one of the three Better Sounding Questions for your Steel Drum Project. Now, break it into three parts, and work backward:

1. By the end of the week, what do you want to have accomplished? We call this, "What's the TaDa!?"

2. What's the first small step you need to take? We call this, "What's the First Crash-Through?" You're looking for the first words or actions, and when you're going to take them.

203

3. Then think about what you'd do in one 90-minute Solo Session to achieve this goal. We call that "Ride the Cymbal-ic How?" Here you may decide that you need more than one Solo Session. That's great. Plan that out; it may also need a 60-minute Jam Session with your team, or a few items to complete in a 30-minute Finale! session.

Finally, determine what will you reward yourself with when you achieve your Steel Drum TaDa! Maybe a workout or nice lunch? Maybe a new outfit, or leaving early on Friday? Write this motivating reward in the 4th Cymbal circle called, "The Symbolic Reward." This puts the Steel Backbone in your Steel Drum project.

WEEKLY BEAT SHEET TO CALENDAR

Now that your BEAT Sheet for the week is done, begin blocking out your calendar with Steel Drum Sessions. Then pick any other questions from your other Skill Drums. Block two Solo Sessions in your calendar per day. It's OK to leave the topic blank. When the time comes, you can improvise off your Daily BEAT Sheet.

HOW MANY PROJECTS TOTAL?

There is a fair amount of controversy regarding the number of projects you should have at any given time. Some maestros say that you should try to focus on one item per week; others have so many they need elaborate software to track everything. Neuroscience suggests we are wired to work in threes, and anything over seven may be counterproductive.

In the DRUMBEAT, you can only dance to the Beat you hear. Take a deep breath. If each of your 7 Skill Drums has three items, and your Steel Drum has three, that's a total of twenty-four items. But remember, you can only work on one at a time.

Based on two sets per day, five days per week, and three sessions each, you will eventually be able to spend quality time with over thirty per week. And you may really only need eight—one in each Skill Drum and a Steel Drum project. But it's not about quantity. It's about winning!

At the end of the day, it boils down to your style, the style of the boss, and your personal focus and drive. Remember, out of the dozens or hundreds of Notes in your Kettle Drum, it takes a lot to determine the one challenge or opportunity that's worthy of your attention and skills. Play these drums until it becomes evident that you need to abandon one of the projects for another.

Supremely productive people are usually so caught up with their projects they're always looking for new interesting ones. People who aren't productive, on the other hand, suffer from Parkinson's Law.

"WORK EXPANDS SO AS TO FILL THE TIME
AVAILABLE FOR ITS COMPLETION."
—*Cyril Northcote Parkinson*

On a scale of 1 to 5 (1 is when your Band of Characters is always trying to get you to catch up to their Beat, and 5 is when you are caught up and looking for winning things to do) what's your Beat? Why is anything under 4 acceptable?

SMALL "S" STRATEGIES

We'll cover more on this topic in the next chapter on Trio styles, but now let's look at some personal DRUMBEAT strategies. We'll stick with four tunes.

\ Your projects
\ Your Band of Characters' projects
\ Your team's projects
\ Your company's projects

Other people's projects may require you to schedule a 90-minute, 60-minute, 30-minute, or 4-minute session. Each week you have at least ten Sets comprised of thirty sessions, plus some improvisation time each day. You'll be amazed at what you can knock out in the time a song can be sung.

Tip: If you can't catch the Beat in four minutes, move on to a different project that interests you.

By using simple math, you might be able to cover each of the four tunes above in as little as one Set or in at most two days, assuming they all require a 90-minute Solo Session.

TWO-DAY DRUMBEAT DEFAULT

Now, a two-day DRUMBEAT may be too fast or too slow to find harmony with your fellow drummers. But it's a good default starting point, and you can adjust it as needed. What does this look like? When asked, "When can I have that?" test this default with "by 5pm tomorrow." Then find a Session that you can devote to it.

How will you know if your BEAT Sheet strategy is working? Use the scale above. When you are about to start a new Session and see that everything is already on track, give yourself a 5; you're on your way to being a maestro. In the words of possibly the greatest Beat Virtuoso ever . . .

"WE DON'T KNOW THE POWER THAT'S
WITHIN OUR OWN BODIES."

—*Dave Brubeck*

THE WEEK, THE DAY, AND YOU

So, what if you're crushing your week and need more Beats for your drums? You can always pull the next Beat out of one of the 7 Skill Drums. If those are done, take a look at your Better Sounding Questions and see if any are ready for some Beats. Then try the Notes in the bottom of the Kettle and see if you can promote any through your Filtering Questions. You may connect an answer you found months ago to a challenge you didn't yet know you had. These things happen when you've got a complete productivity system.

The two 3-hour Sets per day leave you about 2 hours to improvise, depending where the day is leading you. This largely depends on your style, the boss, your muse, and other factors. The good news is you've already had a supremely productive day. You almost can't go wrong.

You can take a few minutes, maybe no longer than a song, and rough out your BEAT Sheet for tomorrow. You can use the sample sheets in the appendix. I personally prefer an LCD eWriter for the Daily BEAT. Sometimes I use index cards, or repurpose the B-sides of paper.

Here are three strategies for that remaining two-or-so hours each day.

1. Let's say you're working from home, and the plumber is interrupting you every ten minutes. This is not the time for a 90-minute deep dive. It is, however, a wonderful time for some Finales!—quick tasks that can be completed in very short bursts. Answer some emails. Pay some bills. Book a flight.

2. Conversely, let's say you're at the company, it's 9:30am and your 10am meeting cancels. You now have the unexpected gift of a 90-minute uninterrupted Session for one of your Steel Drum projects. Close the door, or put up the Do Not Disturb signal.

3. You just finished an intense 90-minute Session, but you're coming up blank. Take a walk or a 4-minute exercise break. If you still can't find your muse, here are a couple of ideas. Pick the easiest thing in your Finale! Drum and try to complete that. Or pick a communication task like a phone call that will be a pleasure to make and that hasn't got much risk attached to it, just in case you're a bit off tune. I've found that a good phone call can reboot an entire day.

If you can't get two 90-minute Solo Sessions or a complete Set in during the day, then you might consider getting up earlier. There are actually four parts to the day: before breakfast, before lunch, before dinner, and before bed. When writing this book, I frequently got up at 4am and went straight to my desk after drinking a lot of chlorine-free water and doing a few minutes of exercise or yoga to wake up.

If you have too many responsibilities during the morning, consider grabbing a Set or Session sometime before bed. I frequently skip my hour of reading or TV to write instead.

I know a couple of people who, if they wake up in the middle of the night, put in a Session and go back to bed. That has never worked for me. It is VERY important you get enough REM sleep periods. Your brain needs to repair itself overnight or you'll be out of rhythm tomorrow. But you might try this sometime to see if it works for you. Remember Rule #18: Be a BIG fan of small tests.

COUNTING BEATS

The last item on the Weekly BEAT Sheet is Counting Beats. At the end of your first week, count up how many items have been crossed off and completed. Save your sheets to review occasionally. You'll see how your Beats go up over time. Be aware that deciding NOT to do something and crossing it off also counts as a Beat.

> "THE ESSENCE OF STRATEGY IS KNOWING
> WHAT NOT TO DO."
> —*Michael Porter*

You can also count Beats each night if you are really trying to up your productivity game. After you get in some practice, having empty space on your Daily BEAT Sheet may be motivating enough to keep you going.

REVIEWING YOUR BEAT SHEETS

Reviewing could almost be a Skill Drum in itself. But it's not, because this is frequently done before bed. Banging on a drum and then trying to go to sleep is not a productive strategy.

Here are a few light taps to consider between days.

/ It's best to set the goal for a week very early Monday morning when you're fresh.

/ Do you have a plan for both 90-minute Sessions tomorrow?

/ How well did the 90-minute Sessions go today?

/ What might you do differently the next time something similar happens?

/ If you are unsure of tomorrow's plan, try phrasing it as a Better Sounding Question before going to bed.

/ Then start your wind-down rituals and GET A GOOD NIGHT'S SLEEP!

\

CHAPTER REVIEW

Everything in this book is captured either in the one-page weekly BEAT Sheet or Digital BEAT Sheets. You may prefer to fill in digital BEAT Sheets, or write in a journal using the one-pager as a mind map.

Special attention should be paid to which you prefer for your external Notes, and filtering in the Kettle Drum of Questions. This is where you will begin to make fantastically better decisions.

The Kettle items flow into the weekly BEAT Sheet and into the Daily BEAT, which can be highly personalized to suit your style. But at its core are two 3-Hour Sets per day, each comprised of a 90-minute, 60-minute, and 30-minute Session. You'll be amazed at how quickly you'll catch a comfortable rhythm to your day and week.

\|

THREE BEATS TO REMEMBER

\   The Kettle Document flows to the Weekly BEAT Sheet Menu to the Daily BEAT.

| Practice with the 90-minute, 60-minute, and 30-minute Sessions to find your best mix.

/   Think of your day in Sets and Sessions, and you'll soon catch a comfortable Beat.

\|/

PRACTICE

Individuals

Set your Kettle up! You won't believe the difference it will make in your week after you get some practice with it.

Teams (Your Band of Characters)

Compare your weekly BEAT Sheets to make sure you're all in rhythm.

Large Companies

The DRUMBEAT is about getting your company THINKING! Think about ways to track how better thinking can be measured. Are your key metrics improving? Are fewer deadlines missed? Are you getting fewer customer complaints? Are employee engagement scores rising?

\|//

YOUR BEAT SHEET NOTES

Look in the Appendix and think about whether you'd like use the digital BEAT Sheets, the mind map, or write in a journal. Set up the Pros and Cons for each here.

YOUR BEAT SHEET NOTES

Then think about whether you want to start with the Quick Start Guide or just go for it with the whole digital DRUMBEAT Business Productivity Playbook, from the bottom up or top down. Write the pros and cons for each here.

PART SEVEN

FINDING YOUR DRUMBEAT STYLE

CHAPTER 17

// Trios, Trios, and More Trios

Trios have three uses in the DRUMBEAT Framework:

1. To help you think more clearly.

2. To help you understand how to express yourself to the world.

3. To tap into the magic that comes when three people find the Beat.

As you go through this chapter, keep in mind that every person, every Trio, and every company is different. Ask yourself the following questions:

- What coaching Trios could you put together to up your game?

- What should you look for in a Trio?
- Should it be outcome-based, or to acquire and share skills?
- What do you have to offer?

The TRIOS OF THOUGHT section is comprised of logical thinking and understanding about why you do what you do.

The TRIOS OF STYLES section helps you know when to go with the flow and when to switch styles to suit a different project.

The TRIOS OF PEOPLE section helps you find two other people who will help you be fantastically innovative and productive.

Let's get this party started.

TRIOS OF THOUGHT

Trios of Thought refers to the inner workings of your mind; how you think, how you interpret, and how you process ideas and concepts. Understanding this helps you define your longer-term goals, and gives you some strategies for achieving them.

Are you here for the craft, the people, or the purpose? What life are you designing for yourself? Are you just here for the money? Do you love the challenge? How do you want to live your life? What are you going to have to say "no" to, in order to get what you want? For what will you be remembered? These are Better Sounding Questions for your supremely productive life.

A, B, SEE TRIOS

Mistakes are almost always rooted in assumptions. These premises are usually based in an "If A then B" form of logic. Premise: If I work hard then I'll be successful. Opposite Premise: If I don't work hard I won't be successful. Contrary Conclusion: If I work hard I still might not be successful. In this last of the trio statements we get to the mistake in the assumption, there is no doubt that Blockbuster and Kodak worked hard and they failed. They didn't work smart. Both working hard and working smart might be the secret to success. I'll let you work through the AB trio on this statement and draw your own conclusion.

Our subconscious minds are a million times more powerful than our conscious minds. So hearing a full Trio of Thoughts on a subject allows your Chief Thinking Officer time to help sort things out.

ETHOS, PATHOS, AND LOGOS

There are essentially three ways to make a compelling argument:

1. Ethos uses authority bias, morals, and quotes. It's all about you.

2. Pathos uses emotion, empathy, and stories. It's all about connecting with your audience.

3. Logos invokes words, logic, and statistics. It's all about the content.

Next time you watch a TED talk, notice that the speakers employ Ethos, Pathos, and Logos. Next time you listen to someone you admire, notice how they present. They're probably using Ethos, Pathos, and Logos.

If you want to be a master drummer of your productivity, you'll use all three too.

RIDER, ELEPHANT, AND PATH

In this Trio, the somewhat small Rider is analytical, the Elephant is emotional and difficult to steer, and the Path is a specific set of actions. This is a mental model invented by Jonathan Haight and expanded upon by Chip and Dan Heath, authors of *SWITCH: How to Change Things When Change is Hard.*

If you want to affect change, you must consider the whole Trio. Think of yourself as the Rider, the Company as the Elephant, and Winning as the Path!

It's easier to get the Elephant happily swaying to a better Beat than fruitlessly trying to steer.

TRIOS OF STYLES

Many management books focus on one particular work style. The problem? That particular style might not be yours. We previously discussed the Snowball's vertical style, the Tornado's whiplash style, and the Juggler's improv style.

But as in music, there is virtually an infinite number of styles. Interestingly, many theories present them in threes. And like a master studio musician who can play different styles, a master drummer can pick and choose between these—and match them to the needed Session work.

You may not own a business, but you do own your career. You may be a blend of these types, but one style is probably dominant.

INTRODUCTS, EXTROVERTS, AND AMBIVERTS

The Trio of Introverts, Extroverts, and Ambiverts are a complicated mix. Travis Bradberry, author of *Emotional Intelligence 2.0*, has written about this extensively. If you have the time and energy to try to help an introvert become a social butterfly at a networking event, go for it. Tools do exist, like the book *Captivate: The Science of Succeeding with People* by Vanessa Van Edwards. But it may be a better idea to send the ambivert (or more reliably, an extrovert) to that gathering.

"SOMETIMES IT'S WORSE TO WIN A FIGHT THAN LOSE IT."
— *Billie Holiday*

However, unstructured meetings are rife for the extrovert to win every argument, even when he shouldn't. A good facilitator or maestro makes sure everyone participates about equally in a safe environment that encourages authentic conversations.

If a thorough report needs to be put together, it might not be a good idea to assign the research portion to an extrovert. While he may be able to get it done, it might take him much longer than it would take an introvert, and could cause unnecessary pain.

Ambiverts have great utility, but they too have a price to pay. Too much "people time" can cause ego depletion, or the feeling of being burnt out. And too many Solo Sessions can cause social skills to begin to atrophy. The habits of balance are especially important for ambiverts.

People usually switch jobs because the boss is a jerk or they don't feel empowered to manage their own areas. As Jim Collins writes in *Good to Great: Why Some Companies Make the Leap . . . and Others Don't*, you need the right people in the right seats for your Band of Characters to jam.

ARTISANS, FREEDOM FIGHTERS, AND MOUNTAIN CLIMBERS

Your stated goals, whether written down, said aloud, or said to yourself are of immense importance. They set the stage for all your other decisions. The Trio of Artisans, Freedom Fighters, and Mountaineers is loosely based on a narrative I heard at a Mass Mutual presentation at a SCORE national leadership conference. Here I paraphrase.

Artisans are business owners or executives who love their work, trade, or art. It is their reason for being . . . their raison d'être . . . their mojo. They are frequently freakishly good at what they do. Some would call them masters or even virtuosos. Truth be told, they would probably do what they do for free.

Artisans often need people around them to take care of the details because they're not always the best executors. Artisans may never sell their businesses, and maybe they shouldn't—but this dynamic makes a big difference in how their businesses are marketed. Artisans usually live life like they are already walking on the metaphorical beach; they believe their life is as it should be.

Freedom Fighters are business owners and executives who have a number in their head. When they reach this dollar amount, they often sell their businesses or quit so fast it makes the final drumroll in the movie "Whiplash" sound like a waltz. The truth be told, they may not even care about the work they do. They may, in fact, even hate it.

Freedom Fighters often want to be doing something else, and may even be working only to support another interest. They may need people around them to stay focused on the softer sides of business so as not to appear greedy. For example, to optimize a sale of the business, processes and procedures need to be documented, and the business must be able to function after the owner departs.

This can be quite a challenge because Freedom Fighters are frequently on a metaphorical refrain of ambivalence; once the money gets good, the impetus to prep the company for sale or get that next promotion loses all urgency. They play on the literal or metaphorical beach frequently, if they don't already live there full time.

Mountain Climbers are business owners or executives who, as soon as they sell their business or leave a job, find a bigger business or job to scale. Mountain Climbers are in it for the sheer challenge of growing and/or selling businesses.

As in Survivor's song "Eye of the Tiger," Mountain Climbers follow their own interests and are easily bored. They need people around them to keep interested in the day-to-day, and not to lose sight of unforeseen changes in market conditions or errors in their assumptions. Because they're moving so quickly, Mountain Climbers can be spread too thin and are often over-scheduled.

TRIOS OF PEOPLE

When you work with two people whose personalities and input improve your creativity and productivity, you'll be amazed at what gets accomplished. Trios of People is also referred to as Trio coaching or peer coaching.

When it comes to people working together, Trios almost always win. A Trio can more efficiently identify errors, omissions, and rabbit holes. Compare this to pairs, who tend to get off-topic or run out of ideas too soon. Four people, on the other hand, often end up in two-sided conversations of two people per side. Five can be a productive number, but it's difficult for everyone to really dig in if time is short.

"WHEN I JOINED THE TRIO, IT WAS AS IF I WAS CAPABLE OF DRIVING A SPORTS CAR AT 60, BUT RAY BROWN AND OSCAR PETERSON JUST KEPT PRESSING THE PEDAL DOWN, AND I WAS TRYING TO CONTROL THE CAR AT 80!"
— *Barney Kessel*

In this quote, Kessel tells how he had to amp up his guitar game to keep up with Ray's bass and Oscar's keyboard. The sum of the three was greater than its parts. Big time. They were challenging each other, supporting each other. In other words, they were coaching one another.

Here are some modern day Trios to consider for your workplace:

DIGITAL NATIVE, EMOTIONAL GENIUS, AND RAINMAKER

What do these three have to learn from each other? Team members who grew up with technology can help digital immigrants who are new to these tech parts by showing them around a bit. The members who are emotionally intelligent can help the nerds and Type As strew fewer unintentionally disgruntled folk in their wake. Rainmakers can help break the drought for their monetarily-challenged side-men and side-women.

Putting strength-based coaching up against strength-acquisition coaching, the winner is unclear. But looking at both methods is a way into a conversation about how you and your team members can make the company more successful. Trio coaching demonstrates both strength-based and skill-acquisition coaching. And it has the added benefit of being distributed across your company; it creates a culture of best practice.

EXPERT, PARTICIPATIVE, AND CHARISMATIC

In *True Alignment: Linking Company Culture with Customer Needs for Extraordinary Results*, author and Vistage speaker Edgar Papke proposes three leadership styles: the Expert, the Participative, and the Charismatic.

I find a most useful application of this theory is in larger organizations with departments of differing styles. Traditionally, these differences can cause distress during interdepartmental meetings. That's because these meetings usually require an alignment of company culture in everything from purpose to customer satisfaction, including all the steps in between.

Using some general clichés, which are often true, production departments are frequently full of experts. Jobs are executed in a certain way and delivered on deadline, so they hardly ever have to have a meeting. Marketing departments, on the other hand, need highly participatory creative meetings. No one may have the whole answer, but all contribute a part. And central management may simply need the charismatic leader to state the transformational vision and get out of the way while the A players figure it out for themselves.

The Expert, Charismatic, and Participative have some overlap with the Snowball vertical, Tornado's whiplash, and Juggler's improv.

JUGGLING SNOWBALLS IN A TORNADO

Let's start with the Snowball. They prefer to get the biggest, most important projects out of the way first. This will likely be a 90-minute Solo Session first thing in the morning, before anyone else is even awake. This method is especially useful if you are a writer. You can get pages done early, so even if you lose control of the rest of your day, you've already won. (The following quote inspired the classic productivity book, *Eat that Frog: 21 Great Ways to Stop Procrastinating and Get More Done in Less Time* by Brian Tracy.)

"IF IT'S YOUR JOB TO EAT A FROG, IT'S BEST TO DO IT FIRST THING IN THE MORNING. AND IF IT'S YOUR JOB TO EAT TWO FROGS, IT'S BEST TO EAT THE BIGGEST ONE FIRST."

—*Mark Twain*

A Snowball probably prefers quiet or trance music while working, with very few words, bridges, or choruses to distract from the task. After the big project is done, then the next biggest, and the next, until all are completed, all stacked nicely like a Snowman or Snowwoman.

The Snowball usually needs to bridge a 90-minute Solo Session with the human interaction of phone calls and meetings. This is best done in a 60-minute Jam Session. To round out the 3-hour Set, wrap it up with a 30-minute Finales! Session for knocking out some quick tasks.

Jugglers prefer all that jazz to be up in the air. Jugglers rarely drop anything—but their act can be distracting to those around them. . . . One minute they're working on this, the next minute that, and "look out!"—here comes another new idea. The crucial difference between the Juggler and shiny-object followers is that the Juggler gets the job done.

The Juggler probably likes jazzy music with lots of improvisation. We now know that the human mind likes to switch subjects, and the Juggler knows that this frequently results in creative and innovative solutions. The Daily BEAT's three Session circles for the Juggling style are just floating on the page or whiteboard any which way.

Jugglers sometimes have too many balls up in the air. It's okay to give it a rest. All that juggling can be exhausting. While multi-tasking is usually impossible since our conscious minds can only process one thing at a time, it's different from the Juggler's rapid-fire serial tasking. (I say multi-tasking is USUALLY impossible because listening to an audio book while on the treadmill, or walking instead of sitting while on a phone call are two of my favorite productivity riffs.)

Tornados like to get all the little stuff done, no matter what, so they can blast through even more important stuff. But it might be a good idea to keep the whirlwind down to a strong breeze. The strength here is that there are frequently very few loose ends on many projects. The weakness is a tendency to shortchange the really important stuff.

In detail-oriented businesses and departments, Tornados blow the other styles away. In participative and distributed organizations, you actually need a Tornado in every Trio. Tornados probably like music with a hard driving Beat. They prefer to start with do-ing rather than be-ing. They're more MET LIPS than LIPS MET when ordering their 7 Skill Drums.

The Daily BEAT for a Tornado has the 30-minute task Finales! circle at the bottom. You can see the pressure somewhat releasing as it twists up into a 60-minute Jam Session for delegating and networking. Then comes the 90-minute Solo Session for deep work, to plan where all this power goes next.

These three types are so completely different, they have much to learn from being in a Trio with each other. Especially useful is that each style excels at certain kinds of tasks. This provides many teachable moments.

COACH, MENTOR, AND PEER

Coaches, in their purest form only ask questions—and not overtly leading questions (like "Why haven't you fired the guy?"). That is, unless it's followed by another question like, the inversion "Why have you kept the guy?"

Mentors provide answers and advice on how to move forward, based on their own experience. Believe it or not, you aren't the first person to experience the challenges or opportunities that come your way. Yes, times are different. But when you really dig in, business is risk and reward. Successful people take more risks and fail more often than less successful people.

Peers have no such restrictions on asking questions or suggesting answers. They talk it through. They question each other's assumptions, look for errors and omissions, and use decision-making models to vet solutions.

Your Trio should attempt to strike a balance of these styles, and perhaps even experiment with rockin' the roles with which you are most unfamiliar.

FINDER, MINDER, AND GRINDER

This model comes out of the services industry. Finders are exceptional at identifying great prospects. Minders have high emotional intelligence and are terrific at relationships. Grinders then do the work that the prospect hires the firm to do.

If you are a solo-preneur, you need to budget your Sessions and Sets so as not to ignore any of these three functions. You might also identify what you do the worst, and hire someone to take over that function. Doing so allows you to have more fantastic performances at what you're really great at—to let the world know you've got the chops.

GIVER, TAKER, AND MATCHER

There is a TED talk and YouTube video of Adam Grant and his work on the Trio of Givers, Takers, and Matchers. Here's just enough information to get you to watch Adam himself: Takers seem to outperform their peers in the short run. However, the keeper of your culture resides with the Givers. Matchers set up a kind of favor economy that can also get a strong Beat going between people and departments. His book is called *Give & Take: Why Helping Others Drives Your Success.*

STYLES AND SOCIAL MEDIA

What bothers me about the explosion of listicles on social media is that they are strictly resource-up solutions, with little to no regard for the top-down strategies of your personal style. When a listicle matches your style, great. When it doesn't, not so much. The best practice here is to be a BIG fan of small tests.

\

CHAPTER REVIEW

There are Trios of Thought, Style, and People. Our minds seem to be hardwired to work in threes. This is quite useful as it avoids the right-or-wrong, one-or-the-other trap. Things are usually not simply black or white; they are more frequently gray.

The Trio of Thought is comprised of logical thinking like testing your AB assumption as not A then B, and A then not B. It seems very simple, but this is almost always where mistakes in strategy are made.

The Trio of Style is essentially how you like to roll. If your style almost always works for you, great! If there is room for improvement, switch styles to meet different challenges, and seek out coaches, mentors, or peers to experiment with different genres.

Trios of People can be much more effective than solo efforts or larger groups because they bring complementary skill sets and expertise to your efforts in much less time. Trios can really jam, and they can be a ton of fun.

The main point is to understand that you have choices. You don't have to be fixed on one style or on one train of thought; there are probably at least two other people who can really help you jam. DRUMBEAT thinking is being open to finding new thoughts, styles, and companions to drive your peak performance. \|

THREE BEATS TO REMEMBER

\ Trios of Thought help you make better decisions.

| Trios of Style help you adopt a DRUMBEAT to match.

/ Trios of People help you get workgroups jamming to a great Beat.

\|/

PRACTICE

Individuals

Pick a couple of areas where your productivity is lagging. Identify two players that could help you. Invite them to a coffee, a lunch, or a party. Have a conversation about how you can all help each other, or start a new project together. Being together more often is the goal.

Teams (Your Band of Characters)

Discussion question: Does our style match the work we do? If not, why? What could we tweak to find a better Beat?

Large Companies

How can the necessarily different styles of different departments be blended together during meetings to create a distinct DRUMBEAT? What can be done to minimize the pain and disruption?

\|//

TRIOS NOTES

Who could be in your TRIO to make a super group?

TRIOS Notes

Pick one of the Trios of Thought to get some practice in on.
What did you notice?

Experiment with a new Trio of Style for a few days, and
see if you notice a productivity improvement. What did you
notice?

CHAPTER 18
// Chops: How You Roll // How We Roll

So far, we've talked about who you serve, why you do it, what tools and styles there are, and when to schedule Sessions in your Sets.

Now we'll cover where to practice, and how to go about settling into a DRUMBEAT style.

WHERE TO PRACTICE

Many people have told me that they swear by having a third place to work; somewhere other than their home or office. They say their productivity is often enhanced by having a third location option for work. And that location doesn't have to be the same each time, either.

I have experienced the same thing. Once I was waiting for service at a car dealership, and I had a breakthrough on a project I'd been stuck on for months. By that weekend, I'd accomplished enough to get that project's website to go live.

If you read social media listicles, you'll see that there is considerable controversy about taking work home and doing personal tasks at work. The DRUMBEAT Framework leaves this up to your personal style. I've said it before, and I'll say it again: Be a BIG fan of small tests to see what works for you and what doesn't.

HOW TO FIND YOUR DRUMBEAT STYLE

There is no right or wrong style. And your style will likely change over time. To find your DRUMBEAT style, do a DRUMBEAT Win Storm: On the top of a sheet of paper, write down some strategies that have worked for you in the past. On the bottom of that sheet, list some times when you were wildly productive. Your style is how to make them connect.

For example, when I had that innovation breakthrough at the car dealership, I would put "Third Place" at the bottom of the sheet. While writing this book, I had the successful strategy of extensively outlining, so I put that at the top of the page. After the page starts to fill up, you may start seeing some patterns which lead to a productivity procedure that works for you. In my case, one of these is "Make outline Notes all week and incorporate them into the outline document once a week."

Using this method, I was able to create and put into action a better strategy for writing this book. I'd started out by writing it the way you read it, from front to back. But when I switched to writing what was on my mind in the outline, the first draft was done before I knew it! The outlining, by the way, was Tornado. The writing was Juggler. And the editing was Snowball.

Go with whatever Beat works for you.

OLD CHESTNUTS FOR YOUR NEW STYLE

Here are some additional useful ways to improve your productivity, work relationships, and level of satisfaction with your daily life. Some of these fall into the category of ancient wisdom, or "old chestnuts." That's because they've worked for a long time for a lot of people.

See what works for you, and it'll become you. There is no greater style than that!

> "NO ONE IN THE WORLD IS GOING TO BEAT YOU
> AT BEING YOU."
> —*Naval Ravikant*

ETIQUETTE EXTENSIONS

Etiquette is the proper way to behave, and Extensions in a drum kit are all the things that aren't drums.

FIRST THE ETIQUETTE . . . HOW TO BE THE BOSS

Don't be like the boss in Todd Rundgren's song "Bang The Drum All Day." Don't be a jerk—unless you've determined that's your style and you're sticking to it. True, it works for some people but usually only after they become ballistically successful. You might want to wait until then—if ever.

WORK TIME IS SHOW TIME

As soon as you set foot in your company's office or platform, you're on stage. Always remember your Rallying Cry, and don't forget to communicate it. A maestro leads by example.

TAKE (AND USE) SESSION NOTES AT MEETINGS

When you are in a meeting, it's a really good idea to write down three key meeting takeaways in a separate journal or portfolio. Refer back to them later. It's a fantastic way to whale on your Learning Drum. Someone has to; it might as well be a maestro like you!

DON'T LIVE IN THE PAST

This is similar to Marshall Goldsmith's wonderful Feed Forward concept. Instead of going over what someone should have done, reframe it this way: "What will I try next time?" You can't manage the past, so why even talk about it? If there is something to be learned, it's a stronger Beat to talk about it in the future tense.

GIVE SHOUT OUTS AND APPLAUSE

If someone on your team deserves praise, be loud and proud! Watch the energy change and the DRUMBEAT grow louder.

AUDITIONING

When considering candidates for a job, consider paid auditions before putting someone on full time. Here's an example: If you're hiring a line cook, pay them to come in and take a mystery basket of food and make something out of it quickly . . . and make sure the result is delicious. If they flunk the paid audition, it will be the best money you ever spent.

HOW CAN YOU ADAPT THIS RIFF TO YOUR INDUSTRY?

My great grandfather played flute for John Philip Sousa. (Apparently, Sousa was a tyrant for quality. It must have worked because Sousa's name still echoes after a century. Apparently auditioning worked back then, and it still works now.)

PERSONAL HIGH FIVES

Many drummers sit too much. I do, while writing, driving, attending workshops, chairing board meetings, and in one-to-ones with clients. My current best practice to keep active is a routine I call Personal High Fives which help me get up out of the chair.

HERE'S HOW IT WORKS.

I keep a dollar's worth of 20 nickels on my desk, divided into four piles of 8, 6, 4, and 2 nickels. The 8 nickels are tails-up, representing cardio, the others are heads up—6 for strength, 4 for stretching, and 2 for warm-ups. If I'm nursing a pulled muscle or simply want to change up the mix, that's ok.

After achieving any small win, I'll reward myself with a personal high five—5 minutes of movement, which is worth 5 Beats. The goal is 20 high fives a day, which translates into 100 minutes—100 Beats. Look at it in any way that motivates you the best.

An alternate method might include the Pomodoro, or the Macarena: Set a timer for 25 minutes of focused attention, and then give yourself a high-five-minutes of exercise.

There is a good, better, and best value for each nickel in my scoring system, within each exercise category. But whatever value I use, my goal is to move all 20 nickels to the other side of the desk by day's end.

E.g.
Good: Five minutes of slow walking

Better: Five minutes of medium walking

Best: Five minutes of brisk walking, or stair climbing, or Qigong walking

Good: Five minutes of stretching yoga

Better: Five minutes of Qigong

Best: Five minutes of yoga flow

Good: Five minutes of pilates

Better: Five minutes of push ups, sit-ups, squats

Best: Five minutes of lifting weights

These are what I've personally tried recently, but...

"THE BEST EXERCISE FOR YOU IS THE ONE YOU'LL DO."
—*Dr. William Sears*

. . . NOW THE EXTENSIONS

It's always good to know what you're talking about before opening your mouth. Shocking! So, before you chime in . . .

THE CHIMES—YOUR COMMENTS

Listening is much better than talking. Before chiming in on a conversation, ask yourself these three questions, courtesy of Craig Ferguson:

1. Does this need to be said?

2. Does this need to be said by me?

3. Does this need to be said by me now?

WOOD BLOCK—YOUR DOOR

This was briefly mentioned before, and it deserves its own metaphor. Open door policies are fine, except when the door is closed! You need to have an agreement with your team about when not to knock on the wood block (your door—whether it's glass, plastic, or a cubicle.) In other words, block the knock.

In the hotel industry, we had a saying: "Don't bother me unless it's bleeding or burning." Wait to knock, don't be a blockhead! Heck, maybe the would-be knocker will make a decision for themselves for a change.

VIBES—THE MOOD

Some scientists are conjecturing that the feel-good brain waves of alpha, theta, and gamma are associated with the human emotions of gratitude, forgiveness, and charity. Would your team be more productive if the vibe was better? It's your call.

REVERB—LASTING EFFECTS

Whether something extra bad or extra good happens, it will reverberate. Is it reverberating longer or shorter than you'd like? If something feels like it's got potential to go either way, try the . . . Whoopie-Cushion—Stink Test

Before putting in a new policy or marketing message, give it a stink test: Think about what a disgruntled customer's, staff member's, spouse's, or neighbor's trash talk might be. They might be right.

TRIANGLE—REBOOT

When the drummer strikes the triangle, it's like a reboot for the ears. When things seem to be getting out of control, strike a metaphorical triangle by calling for a 3-minute clarity break.

Breathe deeply from the belly, clear your mind by counting down from 100, walk around, sit still, or do whatever suits you the best. Then get back to the project at hand.

CHOPS—YOUR ABILITIES

When you strike the drums, you are chopping away at your craft. Chops in performance slang refers to how good you are at your craft. Do you have the chops for a promotion? Do you have the chops to grow your business to the next level?

RIMSHOTS—HUMOR AND HUMILITY

I recently attended a conference whose keynote speaker was Al Mulally, former CEO of Boeing and Ford. Mulally made the point that humor in the workplace should never be at another's expense. Instead, use self-deprecating humor as a sign of humility. This goes a long way in making your Trio and team more productive.

Another note on humility: The Dunning-Kruger Effect is a cognitive bias in which persons who lack skills at a certain task tend to have an illusion of their ability's superiority. Can you see how this could be viewed as the opposite of humility? Don't be that guy. Instead of bragging, here's a default attitude to use when given something new, "I'll try that!" Use your own words.

BEAT CHECKS, DUOS, AND DRUM CIRCLES

Beat Check at 11

Here's a poetic mnemonic to help you check in on your daily DRUMBEAT: The number eleven looks like a pair of drumsticks. If you pause somewhere near 11am to ask yourself these questions, you may be able to salvage a day or even a week with no Beat, and still make it supremely productive.

Ask yourself, your Band of Characters, your team, your company, and your House of Thinking the following Beat Check questions:

\ Are you using your mental models and habit loops, or just working too hard?

| Did you get a 90-minute Solo session in yet?

/ Are you working your Daily BEAT?

| Are you keeping up with other people's Beats?

\ Is there a better way to win than what you're working on now?

| Are you beginning to form a plan for tomorrow?

\ Are you beginning to hear your Beat for next week?

Of course, you can always ask yourself the #1 Productivity Riff anytime you want:

"What should I be-do-ing right now?"

DUOS

You may wonder why the concept of Duos has not been covered until now. It's because Duos are a VERY dynamic collaboration, in both a good and bad way. On the good side, it's great to have a primary thinking parter, a buddy to keep you motivated, to swap a good habit for a bad one, to hold you accountable, and to pick you up when you're down.

On the other side, two people can very easily start work-ing on false assumptions, fall down rabbit holes, and become out of sync with the rest of the team. So, for a really strong DRUMBEAT, it's best to focus on your Trios and your Band of Characters, where the maximum focus and drive lives.

DRUM CIRCLES

You may have seen drum circles on TV, and you may have even taken part in one yourself. But is a drum circle right for your company? Read on and decide.

Who ever wants to try it should empty their literal (and figurative) garbage into the dumpster, turn over their trash cans, and use them as drums. If someone in your Band of Characters is or was an actual drummer, have that person kick it off with a good Beat. If not, you start it off. After all, aren't you a Lead Drummer?

Here's why you might want to try a Drum Circle.
\ It raises your team's feel-good brain chemicals.
\ It's a completely free way to reboot a day in under 4 minutes.
\ It's actually fun and can even be used as a reward.

Here's why you might NOT want to do a Drum Circle.
/ People on your team may be sensitive to noise.
/ You can't turn off the phones for four minutes.
/ Your neighbors will think you've lost your minds.

The bottom line? Test it. If you decide to try a Drum Circle, make sure conditions are perfect the first time. If anyone doesn't want to attend or is sensitive to noise, give them permission to go for a walk. Let the neighbors know in advance. Go outside and leave mission critical staff to answer the phones. Lighten up, have some fun. Play your Day!

\

CHAPTER REVIEW

The DRUMBEAT Framework is a tool, and it's up to you and your team to decide how to use it. Individually, finding a third place to occasionally practice, away from your home or office, can make your DRUMBEAT stronger. Follow etiquette rules for interpersonal interactions, and make note of how your behavior extensions are seen by others. Style is a matter of personal taste, but it is important for everyone's styles to mesh; this is best accomplished by understanding how other people roll. Master these techniques and you'll have the chops for any challenge thrown your way!

\|

THREE BEATS TO REMEMBER

\ Finding a third place to practice can be very productive.

| How we roll has a lot to do with etiquette. Don't be jerks!

/ How you roll is about how little things can make big differences.

\|/

PRACTICE

Individuals

Find a third place to work occasionally. Are you more or less productive there? What kinds of focus work best there? What kinds are worse?

Teams (Your Band of Characters)

Put the "better not knock on wood" 90-minute closed-door policy in place to protect everyone's uninterrupted Solo sessions. Consider dedicating a time or two each day to Solo work for the whole office. That may or may not be effective, so be a BIG fan of small tests.

Large Companies

You might try rolling department Drum Circles. The reaction from the rest of the company might be productive, too! It will be a reminder to the rest of the company to keep the collective DRUMBEAT!

\|//

Chops Notes

There's a lot to try in this chapter. List a few of the Etiquettes to practice with this week.

Chops Notes

Pick a few Extensions to practice with in the near future.

CONCLUSION

THE DRUMBEAT BUSINESS PRODUCTIVITY SYSTEM provides you and your team with a common language for a major productivity upgrade. This will help everyone in your company win faster and more often.

Your competition probably doesn't have a proprietary productivity system. Did you? Here's your chance to grab market share and do the fantastic things you do with more and more customers and clients.

The goal isn't to use the system like a robot. Just get started with the DRUMBEAT by looking at your day not in hours but in Sets and Sessions with your most important projects. You'll enjoy the rhythm, too.

Some days will get away from you. That's fine, it's expected, even preferable sometimes. When in doubt, default to the DRUMBEAT Day. Hear the beat. Play your day.

As you start seeing the productivity rewards of clearer thinking, less stress, more flow, better results, and a happier workplace—play with more and more aspects of the system. It's not about the system, it's about your productivity, your Rallying Cry.

As time goes by, and your players share what works and doesn't work, your company's DRUMBEAT will become so strong that no one will be able to resist your unmistakable sounds of success—your BEAT! Who wouldn't want to play for a Company like that?

Drum on!
Jon Denn

APPENDIX

//Quick Start Guide: The Four Beat
1234 DRUMBEAT Digital Planner

IN YOUR FAVORITE NOTE TAKING PROGRAM, preferably shareable between your devices in the cloud, start with headers for the 90-minute, 60-minute, and 30-minute Drums respectively for Solos sessions, Jam sessions, and Finales! Then add a header for Notes.

1. Menu of Session Topics

\\ 90 Minute Solo Drum // No interruptions.

\\ 60 Minute Jam Drum // Meetings, Phone Calls, complex Emails

\\ 30 Minute Finales! // Short projects, quick tasks, easy Emails

\\ NOTES //

To start, jot down three topics each for the Solo, Jam, and Finales! for this week. Place any other ideas/topics/projects under Notes. This is your First Crash-Through to being supremely productive.

2. Organizing Your Notes

Your Notes may quickly look like a jumbled mess. You have two options, sort them by Project Name or by Skill required. If you choose Skill then try these headers. A+ players use all 7 of their skills.

\\ 7 Skill Drums //

! Learning !

! Innovation !

! Prediction !

! Strategy !

! Money !

! Enchantment !

! Teamwork !

3. Steel Drum Projects for the Week

From your 90m and 60m drums, choose one to three projects that must be done or have significant progress by week's end. Alternatively, you can choose something from the 7 Skill Drums. Either way, these are projects that likely need multiple sessions.

Figure out the goal or that TaDa! for the week, the very first step or Crash-Through, what small prize or Symbolic Reward you'll give yourself when you succeed, and any thoughts on next steps under the Cymbalic How.

\\ STEEL DRUM PROJECT(S) //

(Over 3 is probably counter-productive, 1 is fine !!)

#1 Project: Name it

1st Crash-Through?

2nd Ride the Cymbalic How?

3rd What's the TaDa!?

4th Symbolic Reward

#2 Project: Name it

1st Crash-Through?

2nd Ride the Cymbalic How?

3rd What's the TaDa!?

4th Symbolic Reward

#3 Project: Name it

1st Crash-Through?

2nd Ride the Cymbalic How?

3rd What's the TaDa!?

4th Symbolic Reward

Think about how many 90-minute Solo and 60-minute Jam sessions you need to calendar for the week.

4. All the Rest

Schedule 90-minute Solo sessions to work on your goals, your Big Bass Drum, Mental Models and Habits to try, and your Rallying Cry.

\\ Rallying Cry //

\\ Big Bass Drum //

_____ hires us/me to _____ so s/he can _____.

repeat until you have all your main buyer personas/ avatars completed.

\\ 3 Year Cheer Goal //

\\ 1 Year Track Goal //

\\ 90 Day Rocks-Professional //

\\ 90 Day Roles-Personal //

\\ Mental Model of the Week //

\\ Habit of the Week //

HOW TO SET UP A DRUMBEAT DIGITAL PLANNER (BEAT SHEETS).

If you'd rather skip the Quick Start Guide and go totally sequential, you can copy this template into your Notes program. This template is setup to play from the top down like a Tornado. Or reverse the template to play bottom up like Snowball, or jump around either way like a Juggler. Use this template to make the DRUMBEAT Planner your own!

In your favorite word processing or note taking program or app—set the document up as follows and place your stuff under each \\ item //.

\\ Rallying Cry //

\\ Big Bass Drum //

_____ hires us/me to _____ so s/he can _____ .

repeat until you have all your main buyer personas/ avatars completed.

\\ 3 Year Cheer Goal //

\\ 1 Year Track Goal //

\\ 90 Day Rocks-Professional //

\\ 90 Day Rolls-Personal //

\\ KETTLE DRUM OF QUESTIONS //
// Notes \\ (free form or alternatively consider sorting by Project or Folio instead of the Skill Drums provided here)

! Learning !

! Innovation !

! Prediction !

! Strategy !

! Money !

! Enchantment !

! Teamwork !

\\ YOUR FILTERING QUESTIONS //

\\ Turn Worthy Notes into Better Sounding Questions //

\\ 7 Skill Drums // Sort the BSQ into Skill Drums or your own Project Headers (Hint: A+ Players utilize all 7 Skill Drums regularly)

! Learning !

! Innovation !

! Prediction !

! Strategy !

! Money !

! Enchantment !

! Teamwork !

\\ BEAT Sheet 90 Minute Solo Drum Menu //

\\ BEAT Sheet 60 Minute Jam Drum Menu //

\\ BEAT Sheet 30 Minute Finales! Menu //

\\ STEEL DRUM PROJECT(S) //

Promote 1–3 Items that deserve extra attention this week.
(Over 3 is probably counter-productive, 1 is fine !!)

#1 Name it

    1st Crash-Through?

    2nd Ride the Cymbalic How?

    3rd What's the TaDa!?

    4th Symbolic Reward

#2 Name it

    1st Crash-Through?

    2nd Ride the Cymbalic How?

    3rd What's the TaDa!?

    4th Symbolic Reward

#3 Name it

    1st Crash-Through?

    2nd Ride the Cymbalic How?

3rd What's the TaDa!?

4th Symbolic Reward

\\ Mental Model of the Week //
Keep ones you'd like to try here and pick one for each week

\\ Habit of the Week //
Keep ones you'd like to try here and pick one for each week

WEEKLY BEAT SHEET INSTRUCTIONS
It doesn't have to be perfect. Just get started, you'll have the chance to edit weekly.

1. **Your Big Bass Drums**
   \ What is your Rallying Cry and your core values? What drives you in 3–5 words?
   \ What's your company's main gig? What's your main gig?
   \ What's your measurable goal for 3 years, 1 year, and 90 days?

2. **Your Kettle Drum of Questions**
   \ Set up a journal or digital system to capture all your Notes throughout each week.
   \ Once a week, scan, edit, delete, and sort into Skills or Projects.
   \ Set your personal Filtering Questions above the Notes. Perfect these filters over time.

\ For a Note to pass by the Filtering Questions, it must become a Question itself.

3. The 7 Skill Drums

\ If worthy, place a Better Sounding Question into the most applicable Skill Drum.

\ For now, it's okay to have more than one in a Drum and none in others.

\ For each of the Drums, plan out the next three Beats to play.

\ You will be more productive when you start using all your 7 Skill Drums.

4. Your Steel Drum

\ Promote 1 to 3 of the Skill Drum items to your Steel Drum weekly project(s).

\ The first should be Strategic; the other one or two can be from any Drum.

\ Check with whomever necessary to confirm that this should be your top priority.

5. Your Cymbal Crash-Throughs

\ Plan three critical Beats for the week for your Steel Drum project(s).

\ Put a reward for success or other motivation in the last Cymbal-Symbol.

6. Daily BEAT

\ From the Drums & Cymbals, or your intuition, select Beats for tomorrow's Sessions.

\ Calendar at least one 90-minute Solo Session to ride the Cymbals to a Crash-Through.

\ Place Beats needing meetings in a 60-minute Jam Session circle.

\ Place Beats that can be easily completed in a 30-minute Finales! Drum circle.

7. Each Night/Week

\ Strike completed items, and write down improvisations and new items.

\ Calendar tomorrow's Sessions and start a new BEAT Sheet as needed.

\ Count Beats weekly to measure your productivity.

\ Save Weekly BEAT Sheets to reinforce the progress you're making.

8. Drumsticks of the Week

\ Choose a new mental model to noodle around with each week.

\ Choose a new, good routine to swap out for a bad one. Try it for 4 minutes!

DAILY BEAT SHEET

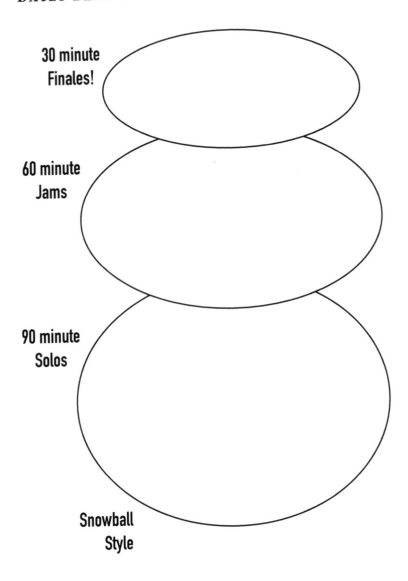

30 minute
Finales!

60 minute
Jams

90 minute
Solos

Snowball
Style

DAILY BEAT SHEET

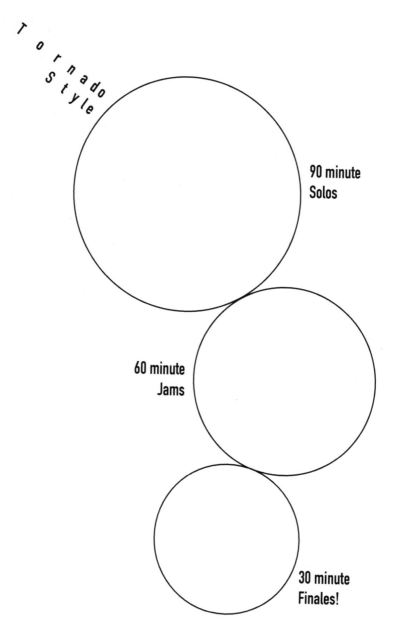

Tornado Style

90 minute
Solos

60 minute
Jams

30 minute
Finales!

DAILY BEAT SHEET

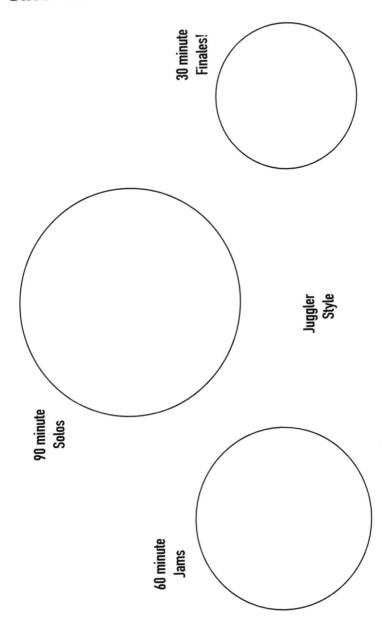

30 minute
Finales!

Juggler
Style

90 minute
Solos

60 minute
Jams

\\ DRUMBEAT BEST PRACTICES ASSESSMENT TOOL //

On a scale of 1 to 5 Beats, 1 being the lowest and 5 the highest:

How confident are you that you can define winning in 6 words or less?

_____

How open is your mindset to new ways of winning?

_____

How confident are you that you do something better than your competitors?

_____

How confident are you that you do something your competitors don't?

_____

How happy are you with your 3-year goals?

_____

How happy are you with your 1-year goals?

_____

How happy are you with your 90-day business/personal rocks & roles?

_____

How happy are you with your external memory device?

_____

How happy are you with your decision-making filters?

_____

How happy are you with your team's decision-making filters?

_____

How sure are you that your team's level of learning will result in winning?

_____

How sure are you that your team's level of innovating will result in winning?

_____

How sure are you that your team's level of forecasting will result in winning?

_____

How sure are you that your strategy will result in winning?

_____

How sure are you that your team's execution will beat budget?

_____

How sure are you of your team's ability to enchant new customers?

_____

How sure are you that your people will enthusiastically act as a team?

_____

Is your team spending most of its time on the most important projects?

_____

Has your team thought out the moves sufficiently to win?

_____

How would you rate your commitment to winning?

_____

There are 100 possible points.

Total _____

What grade do you give your current DRUMBEAT? (A, B, C, D, or E)

"SO MANY PEOPLE DIE WITH THEIR MUSIC INSIDE THEM."

—*Oliver Wendell Holmes*

Remember the win-storm DRUMBEAT !!

123412341234123412341234

W I N W I N

LRLR_R_RLR__LRLR_R_RLR__

The End

 *DRUMBEAT Business Productivity System's Top 5 DRUMBEAT (!!!!!) All-Star Rated Books*

Shift Your Mind: Shift the World by Steve Chandler

Kickass Confidence: Own Your Brain, Up Your Game by Alyssa Dver

SWITCH: How to Change Things When Change is Hard by Chip Heath and Dan Heath

The 5 Second Rule: Transform your Life, Work, and Confidence with Everyday Courage by Mel Robbins

How Big is Your But?: Discover How to Finally Let Go of Blocks and Move Forward in Your Life by Renee Brent

Traction: Get a Grip on Your Business by Gino Wickman

The Five Dysfunctions of a Team: A Leadership Fable by Patrick Lencioni

The Tapping Solution: A Revolutionary System for Stress Free Living by Nick Ortner

Competing Against Luck: The Story of Innovation and Customer Choice by Clayton M Christensen, Taddy Hall, Karen Dillon, David S Duncan

Exponential Organizations: New Organizations are Ten Times Better, Faster, and Cheaper Than Yours (And What to Do About It) by Salim Ismail with Michael S. Malone and Yuri Van Geest

A More Beautiful Question: The Power of Inquiry to Spark Breakthrough Ideas by Warren Berger

Thinking, Fast & Slow by Daniel Kahneman

Farnam Street Blog by Shane Parrish

The Power of Habit: What We Do and Why We Do It in Life and Business by Charles Duhigg

Influence: The Psychology of Persuasion by Robert Cialdini

Pre-suasion: Channeling Attention for Change by Robert Cialdini

Deep Work: Rules for Focused Success in a Distracted World by Cal Newport

Pomodoro Technique by Francesco Cirillo

The Seven Habits of Highly Effective People: Powerful Lessons in Personal Change by Stephen Covey

The Foresight Guide by Foresight University

Collaborative Intelligence: Thinking with People Who Think Differently by Dawna Markova and Angie McArthur.

Mindshift: Break Through Obstacles to Learning and Discover Your Hidden Potential by Barbara Oakley

Brief: Make a Bigger Impact by Saying Less by Joe McCormack

Play: How it Shapes the Brain, Opens the Imagination, and Invigorates the Soul by Stuart Brown, MD. with Christopher Vaughan

Brand New: Solving the Innovation Paradox by G. Michael Maddock, Luisa C. Uriarte, and Paul B. Brown

Predictably Irrational: The Hidden Forces That Shape Our Decisions by Dan Ariely

Inevitable: Understanding the Twelve Technological Forces That Will Shape Our Future by Kevin Kelly

Bowling with a Crystal Ball: How to predict technology trends, create disruptive implementations and navigate them through industry by Yoram Soloman

Make Your Move: Change the Way You Look At Your Business and Increase Your Bottom Line by Alan N. Beaulieu and Brian L. Beaulieu

Mindset: The New Psychology of Success by Carol Dweck

Six Thinking Hats: An Essential Approach to Business Management by Edward de Bono

Decisive: How to Make Better Choices in Work and Life by Chip Heath & Dan Heath

The Power of Peers: How the Company You Keep Drives Leadership, Growth, and Success by Leon Shapiro and Leo Bottary

Blue Ocean Strategy: How to Create Uncontested Market Space and Make Competition Irrelevant by W. Chan Kim and Renée Mauborgne

Tribal Leadership: Leveraging Natural Groups to Build Thriving Organizations by David Logan and John King

The 4 Disciplines of Execution: Achieving Your Wildly Important Goals by Sean Covey, Chris McChesney, Jim Huling

The Fortune Cookie Principle: The 20 Keys to a Great Brand Story and Why Your Business Needs One by Bernadette Jiwa

Purple Cow: Transform Your Business By Being Remarkable by Seth Godin

Fierce Conversations: Achieving Success at Work & in Life, One Conversation at a Time by Susan Scott

Leadership Without Easy Answers by Ronald Heifetz

Culture Trumps Everything: The Unexpected Truth about the Ways Environment Changes Biology, Psychology, and Behavior by Gustavo Grodnitzky

The Tipping Point: How Little Things Can Make a Big Difference by Malcolm Gladwell

Emotional Intelligence 2.0 by Travis Bradberry

Captivate: The Science of Succeeding with People by Vanessa Van Edwards

Good to Great: Why Some Companies Make the Leap . . .and Others Don't by Jim Collins

True Alignment: Linking Company Culture with Customer Needs for Extraordinary Results by Edgar Papke

Eat that Frog: 21 Great Ways to Stop Procrastinating and Get More Done in Less Time by Brian Tracy

Give and Take: Why Helping Others Drives Your Success by Adam Grant

Enchantment: The Art of Changing Hearts, Minds, and Actions by Guy Kawasaki

This is Your Brain on Music: The Science of a Human Obsession by Daniel Levitin

Best Places to Work: The Art and Science of Creating an Extraordinary Workplace by Ron Friedman

Playing it Forward: Because Fun Matters for Employees, Customers and Bottom Line by Nick Gianoulis and Nat Measley

Competitive Strategy: Techniques for Analyzing Industries and Competitors by Michael Porter

The Growth Gears: Using a Market-Based Framework to Drive Business Success by Art Saxby and Pete Hayes

Click: The Art and Science of Getting from Impasse to Insight by Eve Grodnitzky

Triggers: Creating Behavior That Lasts—Becoming the Person You Want to Be by Marshall Goldsmith

Smart Thinking: Three Essential Keys to Solve Problems, Innovate, and Get Things Done by Art Markman and Sean Pratt

Earthing: The Most Important Health Discovery Ever? by Clinton Ober, Martin Zucker

Same Side Selling: A Radical Approach to Break Through Sales Barriers by Ian Altman and Jack Quarles

Language and the Pursuit of Happiness by Chalmers Brothers

To Sell is Human: The Surprising Truth about Moving Others by Daniel H Pink

Book Yourself Solid: The Fastest, Easiest, and Most Reliable System for Getting More Clients Than You Can Handle Even if You Hate Marketing and Selling by Michael Port

Make Your Mark: The Creative's Guide To Building A Business With Impact by 99U and Jocelyn K Glei

Got Your Attention: How to Create Intrigue and Connect with Anyone by Sam Horn

Barking Up the Wrong Tree: The Surprising Science Behind Why Everything You Know About Science is (Mostly) Wrong by Eric Barker

Becoming Wise: An Inquiry into the Mystery and Art of Living by Krista Tippett

Tools of Titans: The Tactics, Routines, and Habits of Billionaires, Icons, and World-Class Performers by Tim Ferris

Unshakeable: Your Financial Freedom Playbook by Tony Robbins

The E-Myth Revisited: Why Most Small Businesses Don't Work and What to Do About It by Michael Gerber

Start with Why: How Great Leaders Inspire Everyone to Take Action by Simon Sinek

The Success Principles®: 10th Anniversay Edition: How to Get from Where You Are to Where You Want to Be by Jack Canfield and Janet Switzer

Hooked: How to Build Habit-Forming Products by Nir Eyal

Stand Out: How to Find Your Breakthrough Idea and Build a Following Around It by Dorie Clark

MINDMAP

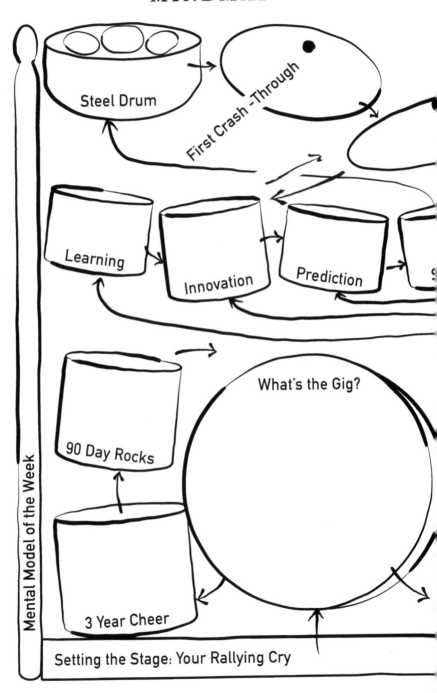

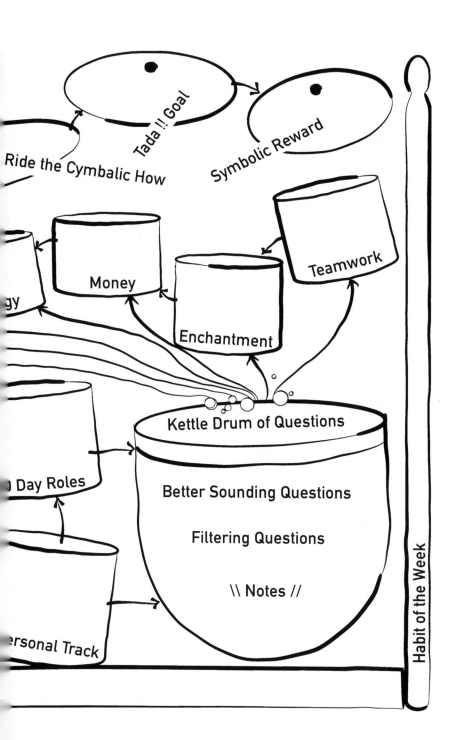

BEAT SHEET PLAYBOOK
\\ MINDMAP //

Steel Drum Project
& Cymbals (Symbolic)
Breakthroughs: Your
4 Beat Strategy to win

The 7 Skill Drums
Learning
Innovation
Prediction
Strategy
Money (Execution)
Enchantment (Marketing)
Teamwork

90 Day
Professional

Rocks

90 Day
Personal

Roles

What's the
Gig?
Jobs to be
Done Theory

1 Year
Professional

Path

1 Year
Personal

Path

DRUMBEAT
PRODUCTIVITY

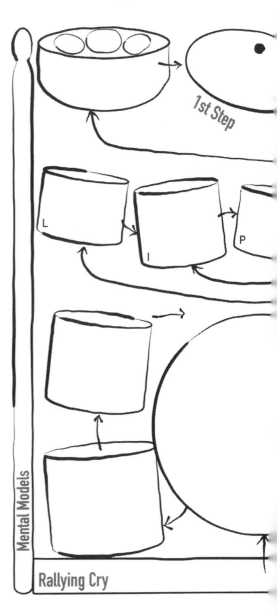

1st Step

L

I

P

Mental Models

Rallying Cry

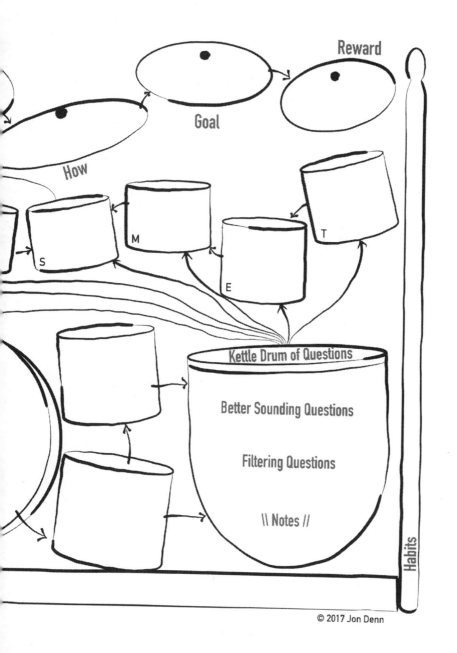

DRUMBEAT JOURNAL

Here's 13 weeks worth of planning pages for ...

Your Rock & Roll \\ 90-Day // DRUMBEAT Planner

The Solo, Jams, and Finales! Menu stays the same on the left-hand side of the spread throughout but there are several styles to practice with on the right-hand side.

When you find the style you like best you can transfer it to an eWriter, paper journal, tablet, or perhaps just use the Quick-Start Digital version in your favorite Note taking program in the cloud.

The point is to customize the DRUMBEAT to your own fantastic personal style.

Your DRUMBEAT default Week has 10 Solos, 10 Jams, and 10 Finales!
Calendar your Sessions by Topic -or- just block "Solo"
Use this as your menu to pull from for each DRUMBEAT day.

"Linear"

\\ 90 minute Solo Sessions //

1	6
2	7
3	8
4	9
5	10

\\ 60 minute Jam Sessions //

1	6
2	7
3	8
4	9
5	10

\\ 30 minute Finales! Sessions //

1	6
2	7
3	8
4	9
5	10

Week 1

am   pm

Monday

\\ Solos //

\\ Jams //

\\ Finales! //

Tuesday

\\ Solos //

\\ Jams //

\\ Finales! //

Wednesday

\\ Solos //

\\ Jams //

\\ Finales! //

Thursday

\\ Solos //

\\ Jams //

\\ Finales! //

Friday

\\ Solos //

\\ Jams //

\\ Finales! //

Weekend

Your DRUMBEAT default Week has 10 Solos, 10 Jams, and 10 Finales!
Calendar your Sessions by Topic -or- just block "Solo"
Use this as your menu to pull from for each DRUMBEAT day.

"Giant Snowball"

\\ 90 minute Solo Sessions //

1	6
2	7
3	8
4	9
5	10

\\ 60 minute Jam Sessions //

1	6
2	7
3	8
4	9
5	10

\\ 30 minute Finales! Sessions //

1	6
2	7
3	8
4	9
5	10

Week 2

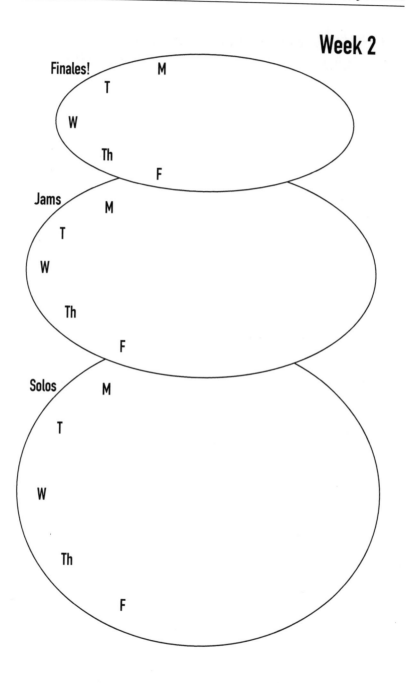

Finales!
M
T
W
Th
F

Jams
M
T
W
Th
F

Solos
M
T
W
Th
F

Your DRUMBEAT default Week has 10 Solos, 10 Jams, and 10 Finales!
Calendar your Sessions by Topic -or- just block "Solo"
Use this as your menu to pull from for each DRUMBEAT day.

"Giant Tornado"

\\ 90 minute Solo Sessions //

1	6
2	7
3	8
4	9
5	10

\\ 60 minute Jam Sessions //

1	6
2	7
3	8
4	9
5	10

\\ 30 minute Finales! Sessions //

1	6
2	7
3	8
4	9
5	10

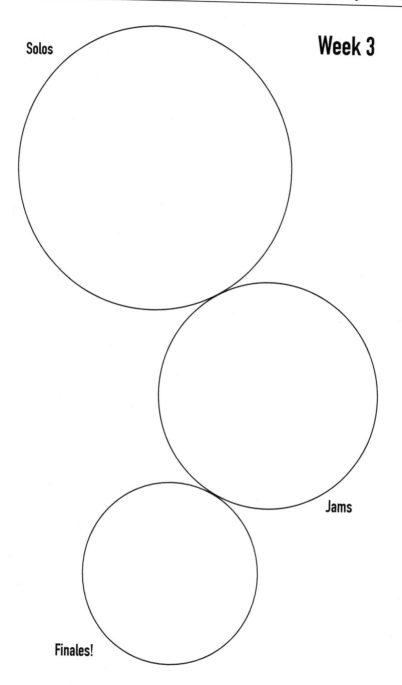

Solos

Week 3

Jams

Finales!

Your DRUMBEAT default Week has 10 Solos, 10 Jams, and 10 Finales!
Calendar your Sessions by Topic -or- just block "Solo"
Use this as your menu to pull from for each DRUMBEAT day.

"Giant Juggler"

\\ 90 minute Solo Sessions //

1	6
2	7
3	8
4	9
5	10

\\ 60 minute Jam Sessions //

1	6
2	7
3	8
4	9
5	10

\\ 30 minute Finales! Sessions //

1	6
2	7
3	8
4	9
5	10

Week 4

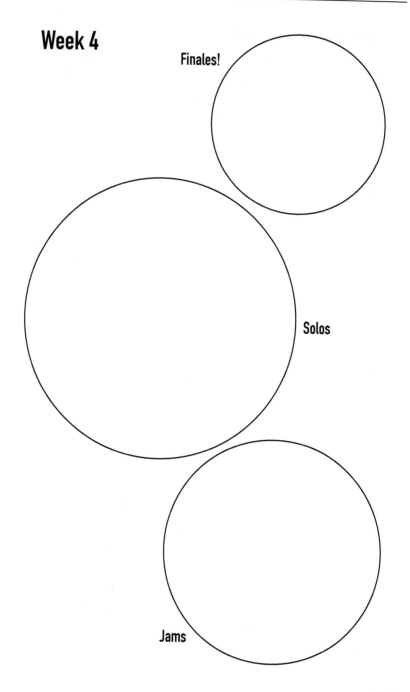

Finales!

Solos

Jams

Your DRUMBEAT default Week has 10 Solos, 10 Jams, and 10 Finales!
Calendar your Sessions by Topic -or- just block "Solo"
Use this as your menu to pull from for each DRUMBEAT day.

Snowball / Tornado

\\ 90 minute Solo Sessions //

1	6
2	7
3	8
4	9
5	10

\\ 60 minute Jam Sessions //

1	6
2	7
3	8
4	9
5	10

\\ 30 minute Finales! Sessions //

1	6
2	7
3	8
4	9
5	10

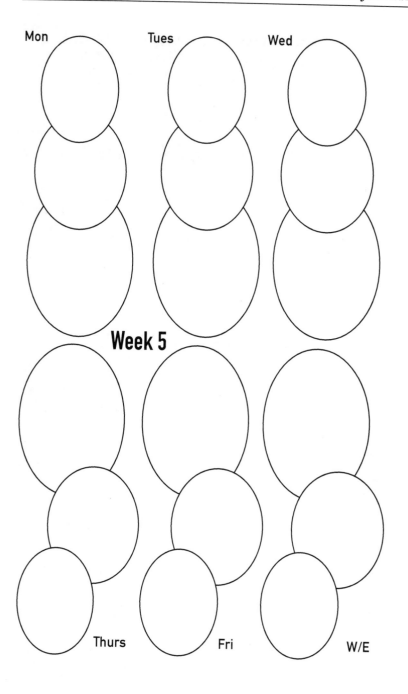

Mon

Tues

Wed

Week 5

Thurs

Fri

W/E

Your DRUMBEAT default Week has 10 Solos, 10 Jams, and 10 Finales!
Calendar your Sessions by Topic -or- just block "Solo"
Use this as your menu to pull from for each DRUMBEAT day.

"Juggler"

\\ 90 minute Solo Sessions //

1	6
2	7
3	8
4	9
5	10

\\ 60 minute Jam Sessions //

1	6
2	7
3	8
4	9
5	10

\\ 30 minute Finales! Sessions //

1	6
2	7
3	8
4	9
5	10

Week 6

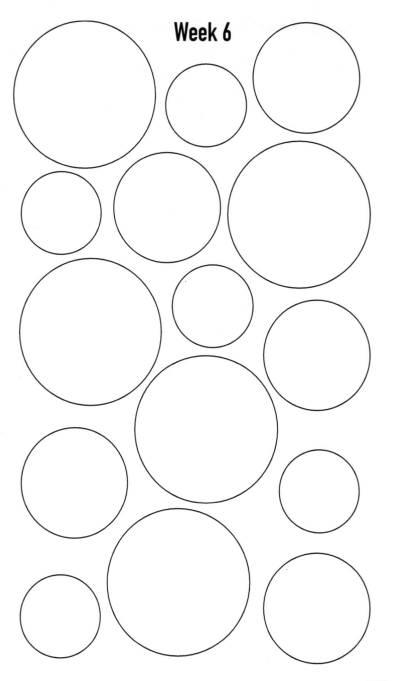

Your DRUMBEAT default Week has 10 Solos, 10 Jams, and 10 Finales!
Calendar your Sessions by Topic -or- just block "Solo"
Use this as your menu to pull from for each DRUMBEAT day.

"Open Space"

\\ 90 minute Solo Sessions //

1	6
2	7
3	8
4	9
5	10

\\ 60 minute Jam Sessions //

1	6
2	7
3	8
4	9
5	10

\\ 30 minute Finales! Sessions //

1	6
2	7
3	8
4	9
5	10

Monday

Week 7

Tuesday

Wednesday

Thursday

Friday

Weekend

Your DRUMBEAT default Week has 10 Solos, 10 Jams, and 10 Finales!
Calendar your Sessions by Topic -or- just block "Solo"
Use this as your menu to pull from for each DRUMBEAT day.

"Open Space"

\\ 90 minute Solo Sessions //

1	6
2	7
3	8
4	9
5	10

\\ 60 minute Jam Sessions //

1	6
2	7
3	8
4	9
5	10

\\ 30 minute Finales! Sessions //

1	6
2	7
3	8
4	9
5	10

Monday

Tuesday

Wednesday

Thursday

Friday

Weekend

Your DRUMBEAT default Week has 10 Solos, 10 Jams, and 10 Finales!
Calendar your Sessions by Topic -or- just block "Solo"
Use this as your menu to pull from for each DRUMBEAT day.

"Open Space"

\\ 90 minute Solo Sessions //

1	6
2	7
3	8
4	9
5	10

\\ 60 minute Jam Sessions //

1	6
2	7
3	8
4	9
5	10

\\ 30 minute Finales! Sessions //

1	6
2	7
3	8
4	9
5	10

Monday

Tuesday

Wednesday

Thursday

Friday

Weekend

Your DRUMBEAT default Week has 10 Solos, 10 Jams, and 10 Finales!
Calendar your Sessions by Topic -or- just block "Solo"
Use this as your menu to pull from for each DRUMBEAT day.

"Open Space"

\\ 90 minute Solo Sessions //

1	6
2	7
3	8
4	9
5	10

\\ 60 minute Jam Sessions //

1	6
2	7
3	8
4	9
5	10

\\ 30 minute Finales! Sessions //

1	6
2	7
3	8
4	9
5	10

Monday

Tuesday

Wednesday

Thursday

Friday

Weekend

Your DRUMBEAT default Week has 10 Solos, 10 Jams, and 10 Finales!
Calendar your Sessions by Topic -or- just block "Solo"
Use this as your menu to pull from for each DRUMBEAT day.

"Open Space"

\\ 90 minute Solo Sessions //

1
2
3
4
5

6
7
8
9
10

\\ 60 minute Jam Sessions //

1
2
3
4
5

6
7
8
9
10

\\ 30 minute Finales! Sessions //

1
2
3
4
5

6
7
8
9
10

Monday

Tuesday

Wednesday

Thursday

Friday

Weekend

Your DRUMBEAT default Week has 10 Solos, 10 Jams, and 10 Finales!
Calendar your Sessions by Topic -or- just block "Solo"
Use this as your menu to pull from for each DRUMBEAT day.

"Open Space"

\\ 90 minute Solo Sessions //

1	6
2	7
3	8
4	9
5	10

\\ 60 minute Jam Sessions //

1	6
2	7
3	8
4	9
5	10

\\ 30 minute Finales! Sessions //

1	6
2	7
3	8
4	9
5	10

Monday

Tuesday

Wednesday

Thursday

Friday

Weekend

Your DRUMBEAT default Week has 10 Solos, 10 Jams, and 10 Finales!
Calendar your Sessions by Topic -or- just block "Solo"
Use this as your menu to pull from for each DRUMBEAT day.

"Open Space"

\\ 90 minute Solo Sessions //

1	6
2	7
3	8
4	9
5	10

\\ 60 minute Jam Sessions //

1	6
2	7
3	8
4	9
5	10

\\ 30 minute Finales! Sessions //

1	6
2	7
3	8
4	9
5	10

Monday

Tuesday

Wednesday

Thursday

Friday

Weekend

WANT TO HEAR MORE ABOUT THE DRUMBEAT?

Good news, there's lots more . . .
Let's Jam!! Here are some options.

\\ DRUMBEAT Productivity Training Workshop Options //
   / One-Hour Breakfast Brief or Lunch & Learn
   / Mini Half-Day Workshop
   / Part One Half-Day Workshop
   / Part Two Half-Day Workshop
   / Full Day Private Workshop
   / By the Seat Full Workshop Event
   / Keynotes

\\ DRUMBEAT Business Coaching Options //
   / Phone Coaching Sessions, 4 pack Tune-ups
   / Online Team Coaching, 4 pack Tune-ups
   / Three Month Productivity Cohort / Tune-up
   / In Person Coaching Days
   / Private Coaching (very limited)

\\ DRUMBEAT Business Coaching Weekly Email //
  \\ Tele-seminars: 24 minute Productivity Riffs //
  \\ Customized DRUMBEAT Playbooks for your Team //
  \\ Bulk Book Orders //

www.DRUMBEATproductivity.com